The Unofficial
ALDI
COOKBOOK

Delicious Recipes Made with Fan Favorites
from the Award-Winning Grocery Store

JEANE

ULYSSES PRESS

Published in the US by:
Ulysses Press
PO Box 3440
Berkeley, CA 94703
www.ulyssespress.com

ISBN: 978-1-64604-124-4
Library of Congress Control Number: 2020946841

Printed in the United States by Versa Printing
10 9 8 7 6 5 4 3 2

Acquisitions editor: Casie Vogel
Managing editor: Claire Chun
Editor: Mark Rhynsburger
Proofreader: Renee Rutledge
Front cover design: Rebecca Lown
Cover photograph: © Natasha Breen/shutterstock.com
Interior design: what!design @ whatweb.com
Layout: Jake Flaherty
Interior photos: shutterstock.com

This book is dedicated to my mom, who introduced me to ALDI, as well as my cousin Julie Neubauer and my sister Karen, who are both long-time ALDI nerds, and my sister Julie, who is a new ALDI nerd.

Contents

INTRODUCTION 1

Chapter One
BEVERAGES 7

Wine Slushie 8

Sangria 11

Berry Lemonade 12

Dalgona Coffee Two Ways 15

Chapter Two
SIDES, APPETIZERS, AND SOUPS 17

Basic Cheese Plate 19

Stepped-Up Cheese Plate 21

Smoked Salmon Dip 23

Guacamole 24

Layered Taco Dip 26

Jade's Jalapeño Dip 29

Baked Artichoke Dip 30

Pizza Dip 32

Roasted Asparagus 34

Roasted Broccoli 37

Easy Au Gratin Potatoes 39

Parmesan Crisps 40

Baked Onion Soup 43

Spinach and Tortellini Soup 44

Pot Roast Soup 47

Mixed Greens Salad with Maple Vinaigrette and Quickly Pickled Red Onions 48

Chapter Three
BREAKFASTS 49

Pumpkin Pancakes 50

Slow Cooker Oats 53

Pancake Cereal 54

Cake Mix Coffee Cake 56

Breakfast Hash Brown Casserole 59

Baked French Toast 60

Chapter Four
ENTRÉES. 61

Best Tuna Melt Ever 62

Shrimp Scampi 64

Barbecue Grilled Shrimp 67

Turkey Meatloaf. 68

Baked Salmon with Honey-Mustard Sauce. . . .71

Baked Tilapia (or Flounder). 72

Baked Salmon with Dijon-Parmesan Sauce. . . 74

Alfredo Sauce 75

Red Pasta Sauce (Marinara). 76

Mediterranean Chicken Bake 77

Chicken Parmigiana. 79

Chicken, Spinach, and Mushroom
Enchiladas. 81

Chicken and Spinach Casserole. 83

Stuffed Chicken Breasts 84

Swiss Steak 86

Pulled Pork Sliders with Quick Coleslaw 89

Quick Coleslaw. 90

Ground Turkey Tacos. 91

Best Burgers Ever 93

Chicken and Zucchini Casserole. 94

Tamale Pie. 97

Cheese Fondue 98

Grilled Pork Chops with Apples
and Onions 100

Chapter Five
DESSERTS. 103

Cannoli Dip 105

Cherry Surprise Cupcakes with
Dark Chocolate Ganache 106

Poop Emoji Cupcakes with Milk
Chocolate Frosting 108

Brownie Oranges. 111

Quick Frozen Yogurt 113

Chocolate Chip Banana Bread 114

Cake Mix Sugar Cookies 117

Homemade Hot Fudge Sauce 118

Chocolate Peanut Butter Ice Cream Pie. 120

CONVERSIONS. 121

ACKNOWLEDGMENTS. 122

ABOUT THE AUTHOR. 122

INTRODUCTION

My mom started shopping at the local ALDI in Villa Park, Illinois, in the early '80s. This was probably one of the first ALDIs in the United States, as the German grocery chain opened its very first US store in Iowa in 1976.

My mom told me it made no sense to spend extra money on brand names. And although she belonged to a local food co-op for things such as whole wheat bread (back then, ALDI didn't have the extensive bakery section it does now) and wheat germ, she bought the rest of our groceries at ALDI. I grew up as an ALDI kid.

Fast forward to getting my first apartment. I had just moved to Milwaukee, Wisconsin, and it was my second job out of college. My job as a police reporter was part-time, so I had to make my grocery budget stretch. Of course, I shopped where my mom had taught me to. Back then, a 6-ounce jar of Happy Farms tomato paste cost about 27 cents, and I remember thinking that 27 cents a can was a steal!

I still shop at ALDI, and today, that same can of tomato paste costs about 33 cents. It's still a steal, and I use it to make my homemade marinara sauce, my chicken parmigiana, and my Swiss steak, and sometimes my 10-year-old son eats it straight out of the can with a spoon!

I have reusable bags in my trunk, I have a quarter or two in my cupholder (more on both the bags and the quarters in a few paragraphs). As a certified ALDI nerd, I know that although I might not be able to buy boysenberries or brandy, I can get everything else on my list there—and I rarely spend more than $150 (and when I spend that much it's usually because lobsters are on sale, I found too many must-haves in the AOS aisle, or my son managed to put 20 containers of yogurt in the cart along with five boxes of macarons). And yes, I know that AOS stands for Aisle of Specials, but everyone I know who shops at ALDI calls it the Aisle of Shame. Because, shame on you if you don't browse it.

A Bit about ALDI History

ALDI started out as Albrecht's grocery store in 1913 in Germany. Eventually the Albrecht brothers took over from their mama, and they turned it into Albrecht Discount or ALDI, for short.

In 1976, ALDI opened its first store in the United States in Iowa. The company's on track to become the third largest grocery chain in the United States, with more than two thousand stores today.

Many of the store's brand name items are organic, and the company has plans to make all of its packaging either recyclable or compostable by 2025.

If You've Never Shopped at ALDI or Haven't Shopped There in Years

If you're new to ALDI or haven't shopped there in years, you might be surprised by your experience. Years ago, the stores didn't have the quality lighting they have now, their produce section sometimes was a bit sad, and if you wanted whole wheat bread, you had to go to a different store.

Quarters—It's Something You Need to Know

If you've never shopped at ALDI, remember to bring a quarter—because you need a quarter to check out a cart. It's an ingenious system—plug in your quarter, get a cart; put your cart back, get your quarter back. Many times, you'll find a quarter because ALDI shoppers are generous folks, but that innovative quarter system means that you'll save more than quarters because store employees seldom have to go round up carts in the parking lot. You'll also never have to worry that your car's going to be dented by a stray cart. Many ALDI nerds have special quarter holders (I just use a compartment in my car).

When ALDI first opened in the United States, they didn't have this quarter system, but they always stocked items still in their cases on the shelves, and they were green before environmentalism was cool, as you have always had to bring your own bags—and bag your own groceries. ALDI cashiers consider themselves the fastest in the business—and they really are. The lines move fast, and once you get used to bagging your own groceries, you'll be out of there in time to get on with the rest of your life.

When you walk into the store, you'll be delighted. Instead of sad produce—a few lonely apples and heads of wimpy iceberg lettuce—you'll find a bright and captivating fruits and veggies section that's really well kept up. It's also, for the most part, already bagged or sealed in containers so fewer people actually touch your cauliflower. Their bagged salads, fresh berries, and avocados are just as good or better than any other grocery store's (including a very expensive one some people call Whole Paycheck), and their selection of organic produce—as well as organic, well, anything—is really huge. It's also a lot less expensive.

Produce isn't the only area that ALDI has revamped. Its bakery and bread selections are vast. From the high-fiber, whole wheat bread that my husband prefers for his sandwiches to the chocolate croissants my son loves as a treat to the gluten-free wraps and bagels I adore, there's really just about any kind of bread you need. And if you're entertaining, its selection of French bread, sourdoughs, and Hawaiian rolls is exactly what you need to put out a luscious spread.

The fresh dairy and eggs are also impressive. Regular eggs cost about 79 cents a dozen, and they sometimes go on sale for 65 cents or less. The organic ones run about $2.50. When it comes to yogurt, you can get everything from low-fat to Greek-style to kiddie squeezies.

Outside specialty cheese stores, I haven't found as big a cheese selection at any other store—think fresh chèvre, Gouda, aged cheddar, Manchego, Borgonzola (a Brie and blue cheese blend), to name a few. Before the holidays, this section grows even larger with other cheeses, as well as prosciutto, Serrano ham, and other sausages and hams, too. And this is where I find a can of fresh crabmeat for less than $10! ALDI also has a decent selection of vegan products—specifically vegan cheeses and milks, as well as meat substitutes.

The meat and fish counter is easy to navigate. Their bacon and their bulk breakfast sausage are so good—their bulk breakfast sausage, I must point out, does not contain any BHA or BHT preservatives, which many name-brand sausages do. (ALDI's bulk breakfast sausage is just pork meat and spices. Imagine that!) I usually head straight to the organic ground beef and fresh salmon—those are regular purchases for my family. But the fresh chicken, pork, and tilapia are also good, and although I might not be able to always buy short ribs, I can get pretty much everything I regularly need for both family cooking and entertaining.

The frozen food section is also compact but perfect for my needs. I'm a big fan of riced cauliflower, frozen shrimp, frozen spinach, and frozen peas. My kiddo loves the frozen fruits, and my hubby loves the frozen, ready-made meals, as well as Mama Cozzi's pizzas (there's even a gluten-free cauliflower pizza version!).

Canned and packaged shelf-stable foods are probably what some people think of when they think of ALDI. Beside that tomato paste, you'll find practically every type of veggie, fruit, meat, and seafood you'd desire. The pastas—including regular, imported from Italy, and gluten-free—are also terrific. And they have a good selection of other grains, including rice and quinoa. ALDI also has a wide selection of tortillas, both soft and hard, as well as Mexican seasonings and ingredients.

Its baking aisle features just about everything you need to bake. From gluten-free baking mixes to cake mixes to really, really good chocolate chips and a vanilla extract that's one of the best on the market, there's everything you need to make the cakes, cookies, and pastries of your dreams. Several people on ALDI social media websites have posted photos of the lovely wedding cakes they've made from scratch using all ALDI ingredients.

Speaking of weddings, I used all ALDI ingredients to cater my cousin Julie's wedding. She wanted only appetizers, and everyone raved about the ALDI wedding. It's easy to garner compliments, given the quality of food you can get there.

Another section of ALDI I love is the adult beverages—ALDI's got some delicious wines, beers, ciders, and even hard seltzers. Seasonally, it also offers some wine-based liqueur-type beverages (think Irish creams and strawberry creams). If you like your wine sweet and flirty, you'll find it, but you'll also find it if you like it dry and tannic. And I've rarely seen a bottle over $20, with most in the $5 to $8 range.

Outside the food items, the cleaning products, paper goods, and baby items are fabulous, but what most ALDI nerds love is the AOS.

The AOS is where you'll find specialty foods—name-brand Pop-Tarts, for example. But you'll also find noodles from Germany, flip-flops, kids' and adults' shoes, clothes, patio furniture, ice makers, rice makers, bakeware, pet toys, gardening equipment, wrapping paper... If you need something special for spring, fall, winter, or summer, you'll probably find it here. You'll also find things that you didn't know you needed.

Most recently, I found individually wrapped cleaner for my sunglasses and a ginormous dog toy that my Chihuahua–Great Pyrenees mix loved. I've also found kid-and-dad matching socks, my favorite bathing suit, a Microplane grater, a monster pillow for my kiddo, unicorn bubbles for my goddaughter, picture books for my nephew, silicone bakeware, a cast-iron skillet care package, an ice maker, and a bug zapper, all of which became birthday presents, Christmas gifts, and Father's Day presents.

It's easy, as I've learned, to become an ALDI nerd.

My Personal Favorites

Besides the cheeses, seasonal prosciutto, and crabmeat, these are my top 10 ALDI items:

- **Seltzer.** ALDI has some of the best canned seltzer anywhere, and I love both their blackberry cucumber and strawberry pineapple.

- **Vanilla extract.** Stonemill Pure Vanilla Extract offers high quality at an affordable price.

- **Canned mushrooms.** I love throwing mushrooms into casseroles, into omelets, and on pizzas.

- **Eggs.** You can't beat the price of 79 cents or less.

- **Guacamole fixings.** I can get everything I need for fresh guac for less than $5.

- **Chocolate.** From the chocolate chips to the chocolate bars to the seasonal truffles, this is where I indulge.

- **Frozen pizzas.** Mama Cozzi's has great frozen pizzas, including a version with a cauliflower crust.

- **Salmon.** I love, love, love the fresh salmon, and the frozen's also pretty darn good.

- **Cookies.** My sister's family adores the peanut butter chocolate cookies, and I'm a big fan of the snickerdoodles. I also love the coconut cashew crisps—sort of a cookie-candy cross that's perfect for sweet dips.

- **Chips and salsa and dips.** Their non-GMO tortilla chips, their salt and vinegar potato chips, and all of their salsas are divine. My hubby loves the hummus and other specialty dips, such as buffalo chicken.

About the Recipes in This Book

Every recipe in this book was made with ingredients bought at an ALDI grocery store. Period. Now, some recipes include optional ingredients—my sangria tastes better with brandy and orange liqueur, and right now, ALDI doesn't sell hard liquor at its stores—but the basic recipes require only a trip to ALDI.

Some ingredients, such as marshmallow fluff, are seasonal, and my chocolate peanut butter ice cream pie tastes better when the whipped cream is mixed with marshmallow fluff—but I include substitution options.

And most, but not all, recipes include variations. If you have a favorite recipe or if you've come up with an even better variation, I'd love to hear from you. ALDI nerds unite!

Have fun and enjoy cooking!

Chapter One

BEVERAGES

WINE SLUSHIE

In Wisconsin, we're big on slushes or slushies, and they're usually made with brandy. But you can make an equally refreshing wine slushie with the ALDI wines of your choice. Although I love red wines, for a slushie, I recommend using sweeter white or rosé wines.

Yield: about 10 servings | Prep Time: 5 minutes | Freeze Time: 3 to 4 hours

1 (750-ml) bottle Moiselle Moscato White Wine or other sweet white wine of your choice

1½ cups fresh lemonade, not from concentrate

¾ cup pineapple juice (from a can of pineapple chunks—reserve the chunks for garnish)

1 (750-ml) bottle sparkling wine

pineapple chunks, lemon slices and mint, or maraschino cherries, for garnish

1. Combine the sweet white wine, lemonade, and pineapple juice in a large, freezer-safe container with a top.

2. Freeze for 3 to 4 hours until the mixture has a nice slushy texture.

3. To serve, scoop out about ½ to ¾ cup slush, place in a glass, and top with sparkling wine. Garnish however you'd like: with reserved pineapple chunks, lemon slices and mint, or maraschino cherries.

Notes

- If you would like to make this a true Wisconsin slush, add 1 cup of your favorite booze—brandy, whiskey, vodka, and so on. Fruity liqueurs work especially well with this recipe.

SANGRIA

This is the ultimate party punch for grown-ups.

Yield: 6 to 8 servings | Prep Time: 10 minutes | Chill Time: 1 to 2 hours

1 red apple, such as Fuji or Honeycrisp, thinly sliced or cut into chunks

1 navel orange, thinly sliced or cut into chunks

1 cup strawberries, sliced

1 lemon, thinly sliced

juice of 1 lemon (about ⅓ cup)

juice of 1 orange (about ½ cup)

⅓ cup granulated sugar

1 bottle La Cornada Tempranillo, Intermingle Red Blend, or other red wine of your choice

¼ cup orange liqueur, such as Triple Sec or Grand Marnier (optional)

¼ cup brandy (optional)

2 cups club soda or seltzer water

1. In a large pitcher, place the apple, orange, strawberries, and lemon slices. Cover with the lemon and orange juice.

2. Sprinkle the sugar on top and stir together with a wooden spoon. Pour the wine, liqueur, if using, and brandy, if using, into the pitcher, and stir together. Chill for 1 to 2 hours.

3. Just before serving, stir in the club soda or seltzer water. Serve in glasses filled with ice and the fruit pieces divided among the glasses.

Notes

- ALDI doesn't sell hard liquors, such as orange liqueur or brandy, so use what you have on hand. Of course, you don't have to add them to your sangria, but it tastes so much better if you do!

- For a white sangria, use a white wine, replace the apple with fresh pineapple chunks, and add ½ cup of pineapple juice to the mix.

BERRY LEMONADE

Made in a cocktail shaker, this lemonade tastes like the kind you get at a state fair, except it also has berries and it's even more delicious.

Yield: 1 serving | Prep Time: 5 minutes

¼ cup frozen berries (strawberries, blueberries, raspberries, or a combination)

2 to 4 tablespoons granulated sugar (see Notes)

juice of 1 lemon (about ⅓ cup)

⅔ cup water

ice

lemon slice, for garnish (optional)

1. Put the frozen berries, sugar, and lemon juice in the bottom of a cocktail shaker. Using either a wooden spoon or a muddler, crush the berries into the sugar and juice.

2. Add the water and shake for about 30 to 60 seconds (without ice, as the frozen berries are cold).

3. Pour the mixture in a tall glass filled with ice. Garnish with a lemon slice, if using.

Variation: You can make this a sparkling lemonade by using seltzer water—just don't shake it in the shaker. Stir the seltzer water into the lemon mixture, then pour it over the ice. If you want a refreshing summer cocktail, add 1½ ounces of vodka, gin, or rum of your choice. You can also top the drink with 3 to 4 ounces of sparkling wine instead of using water and make it a wine spritzer.

Notes
• Adjust the sugar to suit the level of tartness you prefer.

DALGONA COFFEE TWO WAYS

Dalgona coffee has trended hard—in ALDI social media groups and everywhere else—simply because it's a delicious four-ingredient coffee recipe that's simple yet elegant. I've done both the original, which is first, and then I smashed that recipe into one that's got extra coffee and sweetness, and it tastes better than anything you could get at a coffee chain's drive-through window.

Yield: 1 serving | Prep Time: 5 to 10 minutes | Make Time: 5 minutes

BASIC DALGONA COFFEE

2 tablespoons Beaumont regular instant coffee

2 tablespoons Simply Nature Organic Cane Sugar or other sugar of your choice

2 tablespoons boiling water

ice

1 cup whole milk

1. Place the instant coffee and sugar into a small or medium mixing bowl.

2. Pour the boiling water over the coffee and sugar. Using either a whisk or a hand mixer, preferably a hand mixer, mix the coffee, sugar, and water until a frothy foam forms, about 5 minutes.

3. Put the ice in a pint glass, pour in the milk, and spoon the coffee on top. Serve.

FANCY DALGONA COFFEE

1 cup strong-brewed coffee, either instant or another great ALDI coffee, brewed to your expectations

2 tablespoons Baker's Choice sweetened condensed milk

1 teaspoon vanilla extract

2 tablespoons Beaumont regular instant coffee

2 tablespoons Simply Nature Organic Cane Sugar or other sugar of your choice

2 tablespoons boiling water

ice

1. After making the strong-brewed coffee, stir in the sweetened condensed milk and vanilla extract until fully incorporated. Set aside.

2. Place the instant coffee and sugar into a small or medium mixing bowl.

3. Pour the boiling water over the coffee and sugar. Using either a whisk or a hand mixer, preferably a hand mixer, mix the water, coffee, and sugar until a frothy foam forms, about 5 minutes.

4. Pour the strong-brewed coffee and sweetened condensed milk mixture into a pint glass filled with ice. Spoon the instant coffee foam on top. Serve.

Chapter Two

SIDES, APPETIZERS, AND SOUPS

Cheese and Charcuterie Plates

Any ALDI social media group worth its quarter features frequent posts of the most gorgeous, elaborate cheese and charcuterie platters imaginable! As the author of three cheese books and as an NPR cheese correspondent, I can honestly say I've never seen such beautiful platters—even platters at cheese conferences or those prepared by actual cheesemakers!

Although most of my recipes include exact measurements, my cheese plate recipes are more of a jumping-off point than anything else. Take into account your individual creativity, the size of your gathering, and what cheese offerings your individual ALDI store offers at the time. Also, keep in mind the size of your kitchen, as the most elaborate cheese and charcuterie plates aren't just plates—I've seen people use their entire kitchen island as the plate!

Planning

The main rule of thumb for most cheese experts is to plan about 2 ounces of each cheese per guest. If you're from a cheesy place, such as Wisconsin or California, then you might want to plan for 3 to 4 ounces of cheese per guest.

In selecting the cheese or cheeses, I recommend using a variety of different types of cheeses—not just sliced cheddar, Colby-Jack, or Swiss arranged in concentric circles on a plate like some other grocery stores sell in the ready-made deli sections.

Instead, go for contrasting textures and types. In general, don't put two creamy, bloomy rind cheeses, such as Brie and Camembert, together—pick one and then contrast that with an aged, firm cheese, such as cheddar, Gouda, or Manchego.

Usually, if I'm entertaining I pick between three and seven types of cheeses. Often I'll choose a fresh goat cheese or another fresh cheese, such as mozzarella. I'll add a blue cheese and also an aged cheese, such as Manchego or cheddar. That will be joined by a creamy cheese, such as Havarti, and a bloomy rind, such as Brie. One or two different cheeses, such as Gouda or Swiss, or a flavored cheese, such as a jalapeño-laced jack, will complete the selection.

You can serve the cheeses whole. Just place them all on a large platter. Then add the accoutrements, such as a small bowl of jam or honey, fresh or dried fruits, nuts, and olives. I do that when I don't have time to slice or chunk the various cheeses, and it's a quick and lovely appetizer.

Because I'm a cheese-first kind of person, I select the charcuterie, if I'm adding it, after the cheeses and accoutrements. If you are planning on serving charcuterie with your cheese, start with one or the other. For charcuterie, I add one to five different meats, including hams, sausages, and jerkies. I'm a big fan of prosciutto—and ALDI's prosciutto, when it's in the store, is fantastic. I also love Serrano ham, which is sometimes a special at ALDI. Summer sausage is one of my favorites, as is any kind of jerky and cooked, sliced chicken sausages. If you're adding charcuterie, you can also add tiny pickles and Dijon or spicy mustard as an accompaniment. I make a quick aioli sauce—1 cup mayonnaise, 1 tablespoon honey, and 2 teaspoons to 1 tablespoon Stonemill Minced Garlic in Extra Virgin Olive Oil, whisked together until blended and smooth.

BASIC CHEESE PLATE

This is the easiest plate to assemble, and it's perfect for a last-minute get-together or if you just want to treat yourself and one or two guests.

Yield: 1 to 3 servings | Assembly Time: 5 minutes

1 large wedge or wheel of cheese, such as Happy Farms Preferred Cranberry White Cheddar, Emporium Selection Brie Cheese, or Specially Selected Cranberry Cinnamon Hand Rolled Goat Cheese Log

1 bowl of crackers or pieces of bread

½ cup berries or grapes

½ cup mixed nuts, for garnish

½ cup jam or honey

1. Place the wedge in the center of the plate. Serve with crackers, berries, and nuts arranged around the plate, with a small bowl of jam on the side and a knife for people to slice the cheese themselves.

STEPPED-UP CHEESE PLATE

This cheese plate calls for throwing a party, preferably a big one. Although the first cheese plate takes only long enough for you to gather the ingredients in your kitchen, this one takes a little more time. Trust me, it's worth it.

Yield: 15 to 18 servings | Assembly Time: 20 minutes

kale leaves or romaine leaves (optional)

5 different cheeses, such as an Emporium Selection goat cheese (the cranberry- or blueberry-studded ones make a dramatic addition to your cheese plate), Emporium Selection Manchego, Gouda, a creamy wheel of blue and Brie blend, an aged or flavored cheddar, or fresh mozzarella balls

2 different sliced meats, such as Simms Beef Summer Sausage, Specially Selected Black Forest sliced ham, or other sliced meats of your choice

1 cup mixed nuts, such as almonds, cashews, and pistachios

1 cup grapes or sliced strawberries

1 cup dried apricots, slivered

½ cup Dijon mustard

½ cup Berryhill Clover Honey or other honey of your choice

1. Use a large serving platter or a section of your kitchen counter or island. If you are using your kitchen counter, clean, sanitize, and dry it, and then line it with parchment paper (optional). If you are using the kale leaves or romaine leaves, you can spread them all across the bottom of the platter or on the kitchen counter.

2. If you are using goat cheese and a bloomy rind, such as Brie or a Brie and blue mix, place them at opposite corners of the plate or surface.

3. Cut up all the hard and semihard cheeses. If you are using big rounds of fresh mozzarella, slice them; if you are using small ones, just drain away the water.

4. Organize the different cheeses in groupings around the uncut cheeses. Try placing them at opposite ends of the platter or in between the cheeses.

5. Add the sausages, placing them in between the cheeses, and preferably at opposite ends of the platter.

6. Then add the nuts and the fruits.

7. Pour the mustard and the honey into two small bowls. Serve with little dipping spoons next to the platter.

8. Add a knife for any cheese that is uncut, and then add serving forks, toothpicks, or tongs for the other cheeses and meats.

SMOKED SALMON DIP

When ALDI has cold smoked salmon in its refrigerated section, this is a dip I make to impress company.

Yield: 1½ cups or about 6 servings | Prep Time: 5 minutes

2 (3-ounce) packages Specially Selected Cold Smoked Salmon or other smoked salmon of your choice

1 (8-ounce) package Happy Farms cream cheese or other cream cheese of your choice

2 green onions, ends cut off

2 teaspoons fresh lemon juice

1 teaspoon Dijon mustard

1 teaspoon onion powder

½ teaspoon Stonemill Minced Garlic in Extra Virgin Olive Oil or minced garlic

¼ teaspoon paprika

¼ teaspoon freshly ground pepper

¼ teaspoon sea salt

crackers, toasted bread, or chips, to serve

1. Place all the ingredients in a food processor. Process on high until smooth, 3 to 4 minutes.

2. Serve with crackers, toasted bread, or chips.

Notes
- If you have fresh or dried dill, you can also add it. Use about 1½ tablespoons fresh dill or 2½ teaspoons dried dill.

GUACAMOLE

Do you love going to those restaurants where they make you guacamole tableside? Well, you can make your own tableside at home with this recipe for zesty, fresh guac.

Yield: 3 cups | Prep Time: 30 minutes

3 large avocados

2 Roma tomatoes, diced (1 cup)

½ red onion, diced (1 cup)

2 large jalapeños or 6 smaller jalapeños, seeded, cored, and diced (½ cup)

3 tablespoons minced cilantro

3 tablespoons freshly squeezed lime juice

1 tablespoon freshly squeezed orange juice

1 tablespoon agave syrup

2 teaspoons minced garlic

1 teaspoon sea salt

fresh tortilla chips, to serve

1. Place all the ingredients in a large bowl. Using a potato masher, mash the ingredients together. Serve with fresh tortilla chips.

Notes

- To season the tortilla chips, toss them into a bag with 1 to 2 teaspoons of Tajín seasoning (a mix of Mexican chile and lime) and 2 teaspoons of sugar. Shake lightly until the chips are well seasoned.

LAYERED TACO DIP

The secret to this dip is the spicy seasoning mixture and the spicy grated cheese on top. Although you can use any cheese—including ALDI's shredded Mexican cheese blend—I think using a cheese that's spiced with jalapeños or other hot peppers and grating it yourself gives the dip an extra kick.

Yield: 8 to 10 servings | Prep Time: 30 minutes

2 (8-ounce) packages Happy Farms Neufchâtel cheese or other low-fat cream cheese of your choice

½ cup Happy Farms light sour cream or other sour cream of your choice

4 teaspoons Tajín seasoning

2 teaspoons ground cumin

2 teaspoons paprika

2 teaspoons onion powder

2 teaspoons garlic powder

1 cup spring greens or diced lettuce

1 cup diced tomato

½ cup diced red onion

¼ cup sliced olives, such as black or kalamata

¾ cup grated Emporium Selection Jalapeño Havarti Cheese or other pepper-laced cheese of your choice

3 tablespoons minced cilantro

about ¼ teaspoon extra Tajín seasoning, for garnish (optional)

chips, to serve

1. Place the Neufchâtel cheese, sour cream, Tajín seasoning, cumin, paprika, onion powder, and garlic powder into a food processor fitted with a standard blade. Process until smooth, 2 to 3 minutes.

2. Spread the mixture on a large dinner plate (or medium serving dish or ceramic dish).

3. Lay the greens or lettuce on top of the cheese mixture. Sprinkle the tomato, onion, and olives across the mixture. Then top with grated cheese and finish with a sprinkling of cilantro. Sprinkle with Tajín seasoning, if using. Serve with chips.

Notes
- If you'd like to add black or refried beans or corn, use about ½ cup for each layer. You can also add a layer of guacamole (about 1½ cups) or diced avocado (about 1 avocado).

JADE'S JALAPEÑO DIP

My neighbors Jade and Heidi have an amazing garden, and every summer, Jade makes this delicious dip for backyard parties and barbecues. It's creamy and slightly piquant—perfect for chips and veggies—and it can even double as a spicy salad dressing. Best of all, it can be made with all ALDI ingredients if you don't happen to have a green thumb (and I don't!).

Yield: 3½ cups or 10 to 12 servings | Prep Time: 5 minutes

1 (8-ounce) package Happy Farms cream cheese or Neufchâtel cheese or other cream cheese of your choice

1 cup Happy Farms sour cream or light sour cream or other sour cream of your choice

1 cup Burman's mayonnaise or other mayonnaise of your choice

3 jalapeños, seeded and cut in half

½ Vidalia onion

½ cup cilantro (about half a bunch of ALDI-packaged cilantro)

juice of 1 lime (about ⅓ cup)

1 teaspoon sea salt

1 teaspoon agave syrup or honey

chips or veggies, to serve

1. Place all the ingredients into a food processor fitted with a standard blade. Process until creamy and smooth. Serve with chips or veggies.

Notes

• If you like it cheesy, add 2 to 3 cups of shredded Mexican blend or Oaxacan cheese. Add two thirds of your cheese to the mix, then pour into a baking dish, top with the rest of the cheese, and bake for 30 minutes at 350°F until the cheese on top is melted and bubbly. You can also add 1 or 2 red peppers if you like it sweeter.

BAKED ARTICHOKE DIP

This is simply the best artichoke dip you'll ever enjoy—it's just so, so good. It's garlicky and oniony and artichoke-y in all the best possible ways.

Yield: 16 servings | Prep Time: 40 minutes | Cook Time: 60 to 70 minutes

1 head garlic

1 teaspoon extra-virgin olive oil

1 tablespoon unsalted butter

1 Vidalia onion, thinly sliced

2 (12-ounce) jars Tuscan Garden Artichoke Quarters in Water, drained and divided, or other artichokes of your choice

1 cup mayonnaise

1 cup sour cream (preferably low-fat)

1 (8-ounce) package Happy Farms Neufchâtel cheese or other low-fat cream cheese of your choice

1½ cups shredded Parmesan cheese, divided

1½ cups shredded mozzarella, divided

1 tablespoon Dijon mustard

1 tablespoon Stonemill Everything Bagel Seasoning

¾ teaspoon paprika, divided

1 teaspoon freshly ground pepper

crackers, chips, or crusty bread, to serve

1. Preheat the oven to 400°F.

2. Slice about ¼ inch off the garlic head. Place in a piece of aluminum foil, then drizzle with extra-virgin olive oil. Bake for 40 minutes or until a knife pierces the cloves easily, and it's completely soft and roasted. Remove from oven, and reduce heat to 375°F.

3. Meanwhile, heat a large pan over high heat for 1 minute. Add the unsalted butter and let melt. Add the Vidalia onion, reduce the heat to medium, and sauté, stirring frequently for 2 minutes until the onion starts to turn opaque and soften. Reduce the heat to low. Let cook for 20 to 30 minutes, stirring every 5 minutes so that the onion softens and completely caramelizes. The onion is done when it is a uniform caramel-brown color.

4. Place the garlic, onion, 1 jar of the artichoke hearts, mayonnaise, sour cream, Neufchâtel cheese, 1 cup Parmesan cheese, ½ cup mozzarella, Dijon mustard, Everything Bagel Seasoning, ½ teaspoon paprika, and pepper into a food processor fitted with a standard blade. Puree until smooth.

5. Pour the cheese-and-vegetable mixture into an 8½ x 12-inch pan. Stir the remaining jar of artichoke hearts into the mixture. Sprinkle the remaining Parmesan, mozzarella, and paprika on top. Bake for 30 minutes. Serve with crackers, chips, or crusty bread.

Notes

• To make this extra spicy, add ¼ to ¾ teaspoon cayenne pepper. You can also replace 1 jar of artichokes with 1 package of frozen spinach, drained, in step 4. Or you can add a jar or can of crabmeat instead of 1 jar of artichokes (stir it in at the end with the remaining jar of artichokes).

PIZZA DIP

My sister Karen went to a party, and she later raved about the delicious pizza dip her friend Lisa had brought. I had to re-create it. And guess what? It *is* worthy of praise—and it tastes just like deep-dish pizza without the crust.

Yield: 12 servings | Prep Time: 15 minutes | Bake Time: 30 minutes

½ pound (half a package) Appleton Farms bulk pork sausage or other bulk pork sausage of your choice

2¼ teaspoons Italian seasoning, divided

1 teaspoon onion powder

1 teaspoon garlic powder

½ cup (about 20 slices) pepperoni

1 (3-ounce) can mushroom pieces, water drained

1 (25-ounce) jar Specially Selected Premium Marinara, homemade marinara (page 76), or other marinara sauce of your choice

2 tablespoons Priano Alla Genovese Pesto Sauce or other pesto sauce of your choice

¼ cup red or white wine

1 (8-ounce) package Happy Farms cream cheese or Neufchâtel cheese

2 cups shredded mozzarella

½ cup shredded Parmesan

chips, bread sticks, or garlic bread, to serve

1. Preheat the oven to 350°F.

2. Cook the bulk sausage and season with 1 teaspoon Italian seasoning, onion powder, and garlic powder.

3. Place in the bottom of an 11½ x 7½-inch casserole dish. Top with the pepperoni slices and mushroom pieces.

4. In a bowl, whisk together the marinara sauce, pesto sauce, 1 teaspoon of Italian seasoning, and wine.

5. Top the meat and mushrooms with pieces of cream cheese, and pour the marinara mixture over it. Top that with the mozzarella and Parmesan. Sprinkle with the remaining ¼ teaspoon Italian seasoning. Bake for 30 minutes. Serve with chips, bread sticks, or garlic bread.

Notes
• This is an ideal dish to serve in a bread bowl—try it out! Although I use sausage, pepperoni, and mushrooms in this recipe, you can add olives, pineapple, ham, chicken, peppers, etc. Whatever pizza toppings you love, throw them in.

ROASTED ASPARAGUS

Once you cook your asparagus this way, you'll never cook it any other way—it's that good. And it's easy, too.

Yield: 4 servings (about 6 to 8 stalks per serving) | Prep Time: 5 minutes | Bake Time: 20 to 25 minutes

1 pound fresh asparagus, trimmed

2 tablespoons Specially Selected Balsamic Vinegar or other balsamic vinegar of your choice

1 tablespoon extra-virgin olive oil

¼ teaspoon freshly ground pepper

⅛ teaspoon sea salt

1. Preheat the oven to 350°F.

2. Line a baking sheet with aluminum foil or a silicone baking mat.

3. Place the asparagus onto the lined baking sheet. Drizzle with the balsamic vinegar and olive oil. Season with the pepper and sea salt. Bake for 20 to 25 minutes until the asparagus is tender and starting to crisp.

Notes

- If you're cutting calories, use the ALDI Carlini olive oil spray instead. Like regular olive oil, it tastes great—just spray it for 5 to 8 seconds.

ROASTED BROCCOLI

Roasting vegetables makes them caramelized and even sweet. Add a little bit of cheese, and you've got heaven in a side dish.

Yield: 4 servings | Prep Time: 5 minutes | Cook Time: 25 minutes

2 crowns of broccoli (about 2 pounds), cut into florets

2 tablespoons extra-virgin olive oil

1 tablespoon fresh lemon juice

zest from 1 lemon (about 1 tablespoon)

2 teaspoons Stonemill Everything Bagel Seasoning

½ teaspoon freshly ground pepper

¼ teaspoon granulated sugar

⅛ teaspoon sea salt

2 tablespoons grated Parmesan cheese

1. Preheat the oven to 400°F.

2. Toss the broccoli florets with the olive oil, lemon juice, lemon zest, Everything Bagel Seasoning, pepper, sugar, and sea salt. Roast for about 15 minutes or until slightly browned.

3. Remove from the oven, toss with Parmesan cheese, and then roast for another 10 minutes.

Notes

• You can substitute Brussels sprouts or cauliflower for the broccoli, and the recipe will be equally delicious. Roasting makes every veggie taste better!

EASY AU GRATIN POTATOES

The hardest part of making au gratin potatoes is peeling and boiling the potatoes—and that's before you stick the whole thing in the oven. This recipe bypasses the peeling and the boiling by using ALDI's canned potatoes, and your family or your guests will be none the wiser.

Yield: 8 servings | Prep Time: 10 minutes | Cook Time: 30 minutes

3 (15-ounce) cans Happy Harvest Whole Potatoes, sliced, or other canned potatoes of your choice

1 tablespoon minced, dehydrated onion

1 teaspoon onion powder

1 teaspoon garlic powder

1 teaspoon sea salt

½ teaspoon freshly ground pepper

1 cup Happy Farms heavy cream or other heavy cream of your choice

2 cups shredded cheese, such as cheddar, Gouda, or mozzarella

1. Preheat the oven to 350°F.

2. Toss the potatoes with the dehydrated onion, onion powder, garlic powder, sea salt, and pepper, and pour into a 7 x 11-inch casserole dish. Pour the heavy cream over the potatoes and spices. Top with shredded cheese.

3. Bake for 30 minutes or until the cheese is bubbly and slightly browned.

PARMESAN CRISPS

If you're looking for a keto cracker or a delicious topping for a salad, these crisps are perfect.

Yield: 24 crisps | Prep Time: 5 minutes | Cook Time: 5 minutes

1 cup Emporium Selection Shredded Parmesan Cheese or other Parmesan cheese of your choice

1. Preheat the oven to 400°F.

2. Line two jelly roll pans (baking sheets with raised edges) with a silicone baking mat or parchment paper.

3. Sprinkle the cheese into 12 flat piles per pan, spaced evenly apart. Each pile will be about 2½ inches in diameter.

4. Bake for 3 to 5 minutes, until golden brown. Let cool completely before removing.

BAKED ONION SOUP

Yield: 8 cups or 4 servings | Prep Time: 10 minutes | Cook Time: 50 to 60 minutes

1½ teaspoons (½ tablespoon) unsalted butter

1 teaspoon extra-virgin olive oil

1 large Vidalia onion, thinly sliced

½ red onion, thinly sliced

1 cup red wine

2 (32-ounce) containers Chef's Cupboard Beef Broth or other beef cooking stock of your choice

2 tablespoons brown sugar

1 teaspoon balsamic vinegar

1½ teaspoons sea salt

1 teaspoon freshly ground pepper

4 slices crusty French bread

2 cups Emporium Selection Swiss and Gruyère Shredded Cheese or other Swiss cheese blend of your choice

1. Preheat a large pot over high heat on the stove for 1 to 2 minutes. Add the butter, stir until melted, add the olive oil, and then add the sliced onion. Keep stirring on high heat for 2 minutes, reduce the heat to low or medium-low, cover, and then stir every 2 to 4 minutes until the onion is completely caramelized. This will take 30 to 45 minutes. (See Notes.)

2. Pour the wine over the onion, and use a spoon to deglaze the onion bits. Add the beef stock, brown sugar, and balsamic vinegar. Stir and season with sea salt and pepper to taste. Increase the heat to medium.

3. While the soup is heating, toast the French bread slices and preheat the oven broiler to high.

4. Once the soup is completely warmed up—about 5 to 10 minutes—divide the soup among 4 ovenproof bowls. Place a slice of bread in the middle of each bowl, then top with ½ cup cheese. Broil for about 2 minutes until the cheese is bubbly and melted.

Notes

- Everyone's stove burners are a bit different. If you have a very high burner, turning it to low will work, but if your burners aren't so high, medium-low might be the better setting.
- If you like brandy, add 1 to 2 tablespoons when you are adding in the wine. It enhances all of the other ingredients.

SPINACH AND TORTELLINI SOUP

This delicious soup makes for a quick and easy weekday dinner.

Yield: about 8 cups or 4 servings | Prep Time: 5 minutes | Cook Time: 25 to 30 minutes

1 tablespoon extra-virgin olive oil

½ white onion, diced

1 teaspoon Stonemill Minced Garlic in Extra Virgin Olive Oil or minced garlic

1 (32-ounce) container Simply Nature chicken bone broth or other chicken bone broth of your choice

½ cup white wine

1 (8.8-ounce) package Priano Cheese Tortellini or other tortellini of your choice

1 (10-ounce) package frozen spinach, thawed

1 tablespoon Simply Nature Organic Basil Stir-in Paste

1 teaspoon sea salt

½ teaspoon freshly ground pepper

Parmesan cheese and olive oil, for garnish

1. Preheat a large pot over high heat for 1 minute.

2. Add the olive oil and heat for another minute. Then add the onion and garlic, and sauté for 2 to 3 minutes, until softened and just starting to brown.

3. Pour the bone broth and wine over the onion and garlic. Cover and bring to a boil. Add the tortellini, spinach, and seasonings. Cook for 8 minutes or until the tortellini is al dente. Remove from the heat and let cool for 5 minutes. Serve with a sprinkle of Parmesan cheese and olive oil.

Notes

• Replace the olive oil with bacon grease, and then add 3 or 4 strips of cooked bacon, crumbled, into the soup. Or add 1 cup of cooked, diced chicken.

POT ROAST SOUP

Yield: 10 cups or about 5 servings | Prep Time: 10 minutes | Cook Time: 45 to 50 minutes

2 tablespoons unsalted butter or bacon grease

1½ pounds USDA Choice Black Angus Beef from ALDI Stew Meat or other beef stew meat of your choice

2 teaspoons Stonemill Minced Garlic in Extra Virgin Olive Oil or minced garlic

½ large Vidalia onion, thinly sliced

1 (8-ounce) package sliced white mushrooms

2 large carrots, peeled and sliced (about 1 cup)

1 (15-ounce) can whole potatoes, drained and sliced

1 cup frozen peas (optional)

2 teaspoons sea salt

1 teaspoon freshly ground pepper

¼ teaspoon ground cinnamon

2 tablespoons all-purpose flour or liveGfree pancake and baking mix

2 cups Stormchaser Red Blend wine or other red wine of your choice

1 (32-ounce) container of Chef's Cupboard Beef Broth or other beef broth of your choice

crusty bread, to serve (optional)

1. Preheat a large pot on high heat for 1 to 2 minutes. Add the butter or bacon grease until melted then add the stew meat and sauté until no longer pink.

2. Add the minced garlic and onion, and sauté for about 2 to 3 minutes, until softened. Add the mushrooms and sauté until cooked through, about 4 to 5 minutes. Add the carrots and sauté until cooked through, about 5 minutes. Add the potatoes and peas, if using.

3. Season with sea salt, pepper, and cinnamon, and stir together. Add the flour and stir on the bottom until completely dissolved.

4. Pour the red wine on top of the soup mixture, and scrape the brown bits off the bottom. Pour in the beef broth and reduce the heat to low. Cook for 15 to 20 minutes. Serve with crusty bread, if desired.

MIXED GREENS SALAD WITH MAPLE VINAIGRETTE AND QUICKLY PICKLED RED ONIONS

This maple vinaigrette is one of my all-time favorite salad dressings. It seems so fancy but it's really simple to make.

Yield: 4 servings | Prep Time: 20 minutes | Assembly Time: 5 minutes

SALAD:

4 cups Simply Nature Organic Mixed Greens or other mixed greens of your choice

4 cups diced or sliced veggies, such as tomatoes, red peppers, cucumbers, or carrots

Quickly Pickled Red Onions (recipe follows)

Maple Vinaigrette (recipe follows)

QUICKLY PICKLED RED ONIONS:

⅔ cup apple cider vinegar

1 tablespoon sugar

1 teaspoon salt

½ cup sliced red onions

MAPLE VINAIGRETTE:

¼ cup apple cider vinegar

¼ cup extra-virgin olive oil

2 tablespoons Specially Selected 100% Pure Maple Syrup or other maple syrup of your choice

¼ teaspoon sea salt

⅛ teaspoon freshly ground pepper

1. To make the quickly pickled red onions, whisk the apple cider vinegar with the sugar and salt. Stir in the sliced red onions, and let sit for 15 minutes. Strain.

2. To make the maple vinaigrette, whisk together the apple cider vinegar, extra-virgin olive oil, maple syrup, sea salt, and pepper.

3. To assemble the salad, toss the spring greens, vegetables, quickly pickled red onions, and vinaigrette together. Divide among four bowls.

Notes
- To make this a fancier salad, add nuts or croutons and also add some cheese. A shredded Gouda, fresh chèvre, or blue cheese will go well with the maple vinaigrette.

Chapter Three

BREAKFASTS

PUMPKIN PANCAKES

If you like pumpkin pie, you'll love these pancakes. They also pair well with cool, fall mornings and coffee served with pumpkin spice creamer.

Yield: 12 to 14 pancakes or about 4 servings | Prep Time: 5 minutes | Cook Time: 15 to 20 minutes

1 cup baking mix or liveGfree pancake and baking mix

1 cup Simply Nature Organic Pumpkin or other canned pumpkin of your choice

1 cup plus 1 tablespoon whole milk

1 egg

¼ cup sugar

1 teaspoon Stonemill Pumpkin Pie Spice blend or other pumpkin pie spice blend of your choice

1 teaspoon vanilla extract

½ teaspoon ground cinnamon

canola oil spray

1. Using a standard mixer or whisk, mix all the ingredients except for the canola oil spray until blended and smooth.

2. Heat a griddle to high. Spritz with canola oil spray.

3. Pour the pancake batter, ¼ cup for each pancake, onto the griddle. Using a spatula, spread out the batter of each pancake—it is a very thick batter so unless you spread it, the pancakes won't cook evenly. Let the pancakes cook on that first side until it starts to puff up—this will take 3 to 5 minutes. You may see a bubble or two, but you will not see the dozens you would see on a plain pancake. Then use a spatula to flip them over, and cook for another 1 to 2 minutes.

4. Repeat until the pancake batter is used up.

SLOW COOKER OATS

If you need a nutritious breakfast for your busy family, then throw this together in your slow cooker the night before, and in the morning you'll be good to go!

Yield: 6 to 8 servings | Prep Time: 10 minutes | Cook Time: 4 or 8 hours, depending on the slow cooker setting

3 cups Millville Old-Fashioned Oats, liveGfree Gluten Free Quick Oats, or other oats of your choice

½ cup Simply Nature ground flax seeds (optional) or other ground flax seeds of your choice

⅓ cup granulated sugar

2 apples (such as Honeycrisp), peeled, cored, and diced

1 teaspoon ground cinnamon

6 cups Friendly Farms organic almond, coconut, or soy milk or other nondairy milk of your choice

2 teaspoons vanilla extract

additional cinnamon, for garnish (optional)

chunks of fresh apple, for garnish (optional)

1. Pour the oats, flax seeds, if using, sugar, apples, and cinnamon into a slow cooker. Stir together. Then top with the nondairy milk and vanilla extract. Stir together.

2. Cook on high for 4 hours, or cook on low for 8 hours.

3. Garnish with more cinnamon and chunks of fresh apple, if desired.

Notes
- For a change, substitute brown sugar, honey, maple syrup, or agave syrup for the sugar. Or substitute chopped, dried apricots or dried cherries for the apples. Or maybe add ½ cup chopped nuts.

PANCAKE CEREAL

Yield: about 3 to 4 cups or 6 to 8 (½-cup) servings | Prep Time: 5 minutes | Cook Time: 30 minutes

1 (9.6-ounce) container Baker's Corner Funnel Cakes pitcher and mix or other funnel cake mix of your choice

1½ cups water

2 teaspoons vanilla extract

canola oil spray

milk, maple syrup, or sliced fresh strawberries, to serve

1. Preheat the griddle on high.

2. In a large bowl, whisk together the funnel cake mix, water, and vanilla extract until smooth. Pour part of the mixture into a small squeeze bottle or into a zip-top plastic bag. Close the bag and cut a very small hole at the end.

3. Spray the griddle with canola oil. Pour the batter out in small dots, about the size of dimes. Bake until bubbling on top. Then, using two spatulas, flip them over. They take 3 to 5 minutes to cook on the first side and 1 to 2 minutes to cook on the second side. By the time you finish filling the griddle with dots of batter, the first dots are usually ready to be flipped over.

4. Serve in a bowl with milk, maple syrup, or sliced fresh strawberries.

CAKE MIX COFFEE CAKE

My friend Kelty, who likes to bake but not from scratch, asked me to come up with an easy yet delicious coffee cake recipe for her ravenous family of four boys. This one fit the bill in a most scrumptious way.

Yield: 8 servings | Prep Time: 15 minutes | Cook Time: 45 to 55 minutes

1 cup plus 1 tablespoon unsalted butter, softened, divided

1 (15.25-ounce) package Baker's Corner white or yellow cake mix or other cake mix of your choice, divided

3 eggs

1 cup milk (preferably whole or 2 percent)

1 package Baker's Corner instant vanilla pudding or other instant pudding of your choice

1 tablespoon vanilla extract

¾ cup Baker's Corner Dark Chocolate Morsels or semisweet chocolate chips or other chocolate chips of your choice (optional)

1 cup brown sugar

¾ cup crushed pecans or walnuts

2 teaspoons ground cinnamon

1. Preheat the oven to 350°F. Grease a large Bundt pan with 1 tablespoon of unsalted butter and then use 1 tablespoon of cake mix to flour it. Remove ½ cup of cake mix from the package and set it aside.

2. Beat the eggs and ½ cup (1 stick) of unsalted butter together in a mixer until creamy.

3. Add the milk and beat until well combined. Add the cake mix (without the ½ cup set aside) and vanilla pudding. Stir in the vanilla extract and chocolate chips, if using. Pour the batter into the prepared pan.

4. Stir the remaining cake mix, brown sugar, nuts, and cinnamon together. Using two knives, a pastry cutter, or a potato masher, cut and mash the remaining butter into the brown sugar mixture until it is a crumbly yet sticky consistency. Spread on top of the cake.

5. Bake for 45 to 55 minutes or until a toothpick inserted into the center comes out clean.

BREAKFAST HASH BROWN CASSEROLE

Breakfast casseroles are my go-to dish whenever I have to cook for more than my immediate family. This one is reminiscent of a quiche, with a hash brown crust, and it's perfect for company. (It also goes great with champagne and mimosas!)

Yield: 10 servings | Prep Time: 10 minutes | Cook Time: 40 minutes

2 cups Season's Choice hash browns or other hash browns of your choice

½ cup frozen riced cauliflower

2 tablespoons dehydrated minced onion

1 tablespoon unsalted butter or bacon grease

1 (10-ounce) package frozen spinach, thawed

1 (8-ounce) package Neufchâtel or cream cheese

12 eggs

1 cup whole milk

1 teaspoon garlic powder

1 teaspoon onion powder

1 teaspoon sea salt

1 teaspoon freshly ground pepper

3 ounces Appleton Farms prosciutto, diced, or other prosciutto of your choice

2 cups Emporium Selection shredded Gouda, shredded cheddar, or shredded mozzarella or other shredded cheese of your choice

1. Preheat the oven to 350°F.

2. Stir the hash browns, riced cauliflower, and dehydrated minced onion together in a bowl. Heat a large cast-iron or other ovenproof skillet over high heat for 1 minute. Add the unsalted butter and heat for 1 more minute. Add the hash brown mixture and sauté for about 10 minutes, until browned and cooked through. When you are almost done cooking the hash brown mixture, spread it out so that it covers the entire bottom of the pan. Remove from the heat.

3. Meanwhile, puree the spinach and Neufchâtel together in a blender fitted with a standard blade. Add the eggs, one at a time, and then add the milk. Pulse until the eggs and milk are beaten into the spinach mixture. Add the spices and then stir in the prosciutto. Pour the mixture over the hash browns. Top with shredded cheese.

4. Bake for 30 minutes or until the casserole no longer jiggles and the cheese is slightly browned on top.

Notes

• Instead of prosciutto, add ¼ pound of cooked, crumbled breakfast sausage, and instead of spinach, add thawed and chopped frozen broccoli. Pressed for time? Skip cooking the hash brown mixture and just stir it right at the end along with the prosciutto; instead of having a hash brown crust, the hash brown mixture will be combined with the rest of the ingredients.

BAKED FRENCH TOAST

French toast is a delicious breakfast, but when you want to make something fancier for brunch, baked French toast fits the bill. And it becomes even more decadent when you use croissants instead of bread, and when you add marmalade or jam and just a sprinkling of chocolate chips.

Yield: 6 to 8 servings (a serving is 1 square) | Prep Time: 10 minutes | Cook Time: 25 to 30 minutes

unsalted butter or olive oil spray

4 L'Oven Fresh croissants or other croissants of your choice

6 large eggs

1½ cups milk (preferably whole, but you can use 2 percent)

2 teaspoons vanilla extract

2 tablespoons Berryhill Sweet Orange Marmalade, Berryhill Red Raspberry Preserves, or other jam of your choice

2 tablespoons chocolate mini-chips

1 tablespoon powdered sugar

1 cup fruit of your choice, such as sliced strawberries and sliced bananas, blackberries or raspberries, or fresh peaches

1. Preheat the oven to 350°F. Grease an 11 x 7-inch ceramic or glass pan with butter, or spray with olive oil.

2. Tear the croissants into bite-size pieces and spread them across the prepared pan.

3. In a medium bowl, whisk together the eggs, milk, and vanilla extract. Dot the croissants with orange marmalade and chocolate mini-chips. Pour the egg mixture on top.

4. Bake for 25 to 30 minutes. Remove from the heat, sprinkle with powdered sugar and fruit of choice, and serve.

Notes

• If you have an orange liqueur of some type in your liquor cabinet, you can add 1 tablespoon of it to enhance the orange flavor of the marmalade. If you use raspberry preserves, you can add raspberry liqueur, and that will enhance the raspberry flavor.

Chapter Four

ENTRÉES

BEST TUNA MELT EVER

Everything Bagel Seasoning makes *everything* better, including tuna melts.

Yield: 4 sandwiches | Prep Time: 10 minutes | Cook Time: 10 minutes

8 English muffins or slices of bread

3 tablespoons mayonnaise

1 tablespoon Stonemill Dijon mustard or other Dijon mustard of your choice

1 tablespoon freshly squeezed lemon juice

2 teaspoons Stonemill Everything Bagel Seasoning

1 teaspoon honey

2 (2.5-ounce) packages Northern Catch chunk light tuna in water or other tuna of your choice

½ bell pepper (red, green, yellow, or orange), diced (about 3 tablespoons)

½ small red onion, diced (about 3 tablespoons) or 2 green onions, finely sliced

8 slices of tomato, preferably Roma (optional)

4 slices of cheese—cheddar, provolone, Havarti, Swiss, or ¼ cup grated cheese of choice per sandwich

1. Preheat the broiler to high.

2. Toast the English muffins. Set aside.

3. In a large bowl, whisk together the mayonnaise, Dijon mustard, lemon juice, Everything Bagel Seasoning, and honey. Stir in the tuna, bell pepper, and red onion.

4. If using, lay the tomato slices down on 4 English muffin halves. Divide the tuna mixture among the 4 halves. Top with 4 slices of cheese or ¼ cup of grated cheese.

5. Broil on high for 2 to 3 minutes until the cheese is melted. Top with the remaining English muffin halves.

Notes

• This tuna salad tastes great on regular bread and without the melted cheese, and it also is a terrific addition to a salad of greens. I'm pretty partial to making it and then placing it in a wrap with spring greens.

SHRIMP SCAMPI

Looking to impress someone with a seafood dinner? This shrimp scampi recipe is absolutely heavenly; one of the reasons is that it's incredibly easy to make.

Yield: 4 servings (about 10 shrimp each) | Prep Time: 10 minutes | Cook Time: 10 minutes

3 tablespoons unsalted butter, cut into pieces

2 teaspoons Stonemill Minced Garlic in Extra Virgin Olive Oil or minced garlic

1 teaspoon onion powder

½ teaspoon salt

¼ cup Broken Clouds chardonnay or other white wine of your choice

1 (12-ounce) package Fremont Fish Market medium shrimp, deveined, peeled, and shells removed (about 30 to 40 but my package held 43), or other shrimp of your choice

1 to 2 tablespoons fresh cilantro, parsley, thyme, or chives, for garnish

1. Melt the butter pieces over medium-high heat, swirling the pan so the pieces evenly melt.

2. Once the butter is melted, add the minced garlic, onion powder, and salt, and sauté for 2 minutes. Pour in the chardonnay and, stirring frequently, cook for about 2 to 3 minutes to reduce slightly.

3. Add the shrimp and sauté, stirring constantly. Turn each shrimp over as soon as it begins to turn pink. The shrimp will quickly cook, and they will be done in 1 to 2 minutes. Immediately remove from the heat, sprinkle with fresh herbs of choice, and serve.

Notes

- If you want to thaw out the shrimp quickly, place the frozen shrimp in a bowl of cold water and let it sit for 10 to 15 minutes. Then it's easy to devein the shrimp and peel off the shells.

- I save the shrimp shells in a bag in the freezer, which I can then use to make shrimp stock: 3 to 4 cups saved shells, 1 or 2 carrots, 1 or 2 onions, 1 tablespoon peppercorns, and any fresh herbs or other veggies that are about to go bad (turnips, zucchini, cilantro, parsley...whatever I've got). I place the shells and all of the veggies into a large stockpot and cover them with cold water. I bring it all to a boil on high heat, reduce the heat to low, and let it simmer for 2 to 3 hours. Then I strain it and I've got stock, which I can use to make shrimp bisque (cream, butter, sautéed onions and potatoes, wine, salt, pepper, and cooked shrimp, of course!). Or I use it with clam juice to make a more flavorful clam chowder.

BARBECUE GRILLED SHRIMP

Two ingredients plus one hot grill equals easy summer dining. Add a side of bagged ALDI salad and/or rice, and you've got a complete meal. Simple and delish!

Yield: 4 servings (about 5 to 6 shrimp each) | Prep Time: 10 minutes | Cook Time: 2 to 4 minutes

1 (12-ounce) package Fremont Fish Market Jumbo Easy Peel Raw Shrimp, thawed, or other shrimp of your choice

2 to 3 tablespoons Sweet Baby Ray's Barbecue Sauce or other barbecue sauce of your choice

lime wedges, fresh minced cilantro, and extra barbecue sauce, for garnish

1. Preheat the grill to high.

2. Thread the shrimp onto metal or wooden skewers. Brush with the barbecue sauce.

3. Grill the shrimp skewers for 1 to 2 minutes per side, being careful not to overcook. As soon as the shrimp start turning pink, flip them.

4. Serve with lime wedges, fresh minced cilantro, and extra barbecue sauce.

TURKEY MEATLOAF

Meatloaf is a quick weekday dinner that usually pleases most, if not all, family members. It's also an easy way to sneak in veggies, and that's exactly what this recipe does.

Yield: Makes 8 servings or 8 slices | Prep Time: 10 minutes | Bake Time: 60 minutes

2 cups rolled oats

2 large carrots (about 1 cup), grated

1 Vidalia onion (about 1 cup), grated

2 eggs

2 (1-pound, 3-ounce) packages Kirkwood ground turkey or other ground turkey of your choice

2 tablespoons Dijon mustard

2 teaspoons sea salt

1 teaspoon freshly ground pepper

1 cup tomato sauce, barbecue sauce, or ketchup

1. Preheat the oven to 350°F.

2. Combine all the ingredients, except for the tomato sauce, and mold the mixture into a loaf pan. Spread the tomato sauce on top.

3. Bake for 1 hour or until the meat is completely cooked through.

Notes
• If you don't have time to grate the onion, you can substitute about ¼ cup dehydrated minced onion. You can also substitute frozen riced cauliflower or shredded zucchini for the carrots.

BAKED SALMON WITH HONEY-MUSTARD SAUCE

This is a quick and easy weekday dinner. Add some instant rice or noodles and the roasted asparagus from page 34, and you've got a meal in less than 30 minutes that's both delectable and nutritious.

Yield: 5 servings | Prep Time: 5 minutes | Cook Time: 15 minutes

1 pound Fremont Fish Market frozen, boneless salmon filets, thawed (about 5 to a package), or other salmon of your choice

2 tablespoons honey

2 tablespoons Stonemill Dijon mustard or other Dijon mustard of your choice

1 tablespoon extra-virgin olive oil

1 tablespoon fresh lemon juice

½ teaspoon garlic powder

1 teaspoon onion powder

¼ teaspoon freshly ground pepper

¼ teaspoon sea salt

5 slices fresh lemon (optional)

1 tablespoon fresh dill (optional)

1. Preheat the oven to 400°F.

2. Line a cookie sheet with aluminum foil or a silicone baking mat. Lay the salmon filets on top.

3. In a small bowl, whisk together the honey, Dijon mustard, olive oil, lemon juice, garlic powder, onion powder, pepper, and sea salt. Pour the honey mixture over the salmon filets. Top with lemon slices and sprinkle with fresh dill, if using.

4. Bake for about 15 minutes or until the salmon is flaky and opaque and registers an internal temperature of 145°F.

Notes

- If you don't like fish, you can substitute boneless, skinless chicken breasts, but you will need to cook them for at least 30 minutes or until they are no longer pink inside and cooked to an internal temperature of 165°F.
- You can double the recipe for the honey-mustard sauce, heat it for 2 minutes in the microwave, and then serve it alongside salmon filets or vegetables.

BAKED TILAPIA (OR FLOUNDER)

I love ALDI's seafood. Some is fresh and some is freshly frozen. Usually, ALDI stocks both salmon and at least one kind of whitefish filets. Use either tilapia or flounder in this recipe—both are tasty. Serve with lemon slices and roasted asparagus (page 34).

Yield: 4 or 5 servings (each package contains 4 or 5 filets) | Prep Time: 5 minutes | Cook Time: 10 to 12 minutes

1 pound Fremont Fish Market frozen tilapia or flounder filets, thawed, or other frozen whitefish of your choice

3 tablespoons unsalted butter, softened

zest of 1 lemon (about 1 tablespoon)

2 teaspoons fresh lemon juice

½ teaspoon garlic salt

½ teaspoon Stonemill Minced Garlic in Extra Virgin Olive Oil or minced garlic

1. Preheat the oven to 375°F.

2. Line a cookie sheet with aluminum foil or a silicone baking mat.

3. Lay the filets onto the cookie sheet.

4. In a small bowl, use a fork to whisk together the butter, lemon zest, lemon juice, garlic salt, and minced garlic. Spread the marinade over the filets.

5. Bake for 10 to 12 minutes until the fish is flaky and opaque and registers an internal temperature of 145°F.

Notes

- Microplanes and silicone baking mats are two of my favorite cooking tools—and sometimes you can find them in the AOS section of ALDI. Microplanes are fantastic for zesting citrus, grating cheese, or grating chocolate. Silicone baking mats are perfect for baking—whether it's fish or cookies.

- If you haven't got the time to soften your butter at room temperature, stick the 3 tablespoons of butter in a microwave-safe dish and nuke it for 15 seconds. This is just long enough to soften the butter for mixing.

BAKED SALMON WITH DIJON-PARMESAN SAUCE

I owe the genesis of this recipe to my former boss at the YMCA, Kim. She mentored me as a water aerobics instructor, and she also taught me this straightforward combination of awesomeness for a quick weekday salmon recipe.

Yield: 6 servings | Prep Time: 5 minutes | Cook Time: 30 minutes

⅓ cup Burman's Dijon mustard or other Dijon mustard of your choice

⅓ cup Burman's mayonnaise or other mayonnaise of your choice

⅓ cup grated Parmesan cheese

¾ teaspoon freshly ground pepper

2 pounds Fresh Never Frozen Atlantic Salmon or other fresh salmon of your choice

½ teaspoon paprika

2 green onions, thinly sliced

1. Preheat the oven to 375°F.

2. In a medium bowl, whisk together the mustard, mayonnaise, Parmesan, and pepper.

3. Lay the salmon filet on a cookie sheet lined with aluminum foil or a silicone baking mat. Spread the sauce on top of the salmon using a spatula. Sprinkle paprika on top.

4. Bake for 30 minutes. Remove from the oven and sprinkle green onions on top.

Notes

- Although Burman's is the ALDI brand of mayonnaise, I know that some ALDIs in different parts of the United States also sometimes sell Hellmann's and Duke's, and I know mayo lovers who have very strong opinions about those two brands. Use whatever brand you prefer.

- If you have fresh dill from your garden or dried dill in your cupboard, you can also sprinkle that on top of the salmon (about 1 teaspoon fresh or ½ teaspoon dried).

- You can slice up a package of two zucchini, season with salt and pepper, add some sauce on top, and bake the veggies with the salmon for a complete meal.

ALFREDO SAUCE

Forget that gooey white stuff in a jar. Fresh, homemade alfredo sauce is what dreams are made of—and it's just marginally harder than opening up a jar!

Yield: 6 to 8 servings (¼ to ⅓ cup of sauce per serving) |
Prep Time: 5 minutes | Cook Time: 25 minutes

½ stick unsalted butter (4 tablespoons)

1 pint heavy cream

1 cup grated Emporium Selection Parmesan Cheese or other Parmesan cheese of your choice

½ teaspoon ground nutmeg

¼ teaspoon sea salt

⅛ teaspoon freshly ground pepper

1 pound pasta, cooked according to package directions

1. In a medium saucepan, melt the butter over medium-high heat.

2. Stir in the heavy cream and grated Parmesan cheese. Keep stirring until the cheese is melted, and then reduce the heat to medium-low.

3. Season with the nutmeg, sea salt, and pepper, and keep stirring until the sauce coats the back of a wooden spoon and you can draw your finger through it, about 20 minutes. Serve with cooked pasta and additional Parmesan cheese, if desired.

Notes

- This sauce goes great with spaghetti and angel hair pasta, but it's also excellent over Kirkwood Breaded Chicken Breast Fillets (red bag chicken). It's fun to mix this sauce with Red Pasta Sauce (page 76) when making Chicken Parmigiana. It's also awesome for lasagnas, and if you replace the Parmesan with cheddar, you've got yourself a splendid base for a sinful mac 'n' cheese.

RED PASTA SAUCE (MARINARA)

The ready-made jars of pasta sauce at ALDI are great, but it's almost as effortless to make your own pasta sauce, and this sauce causes both of my brothers-in-law to swoon. Plus, I've got two variations that have you covered if you like meat or 'shrooms.

Yield: about 8 cups or 8 servings | Prep Time: 10 minutes | Cook Time: 25 to 37 minutes

1 tablespoon unsalted butter

2 teaspoons extra-virgin olive oil

1 medium Vidalia onion, minced

2 teaspoons Stonemill Minced Garlic in Extra Virgin Olive Oil or minced garlic

1 cup Winking Owl Cabernet Sauvignon or other dry red wine of your choice

2 (28-ounce) cans Happy Harvest crushed tomatoes or other tomatoes of your choice

1 (6-ounce) can Happy Harvest tomato paste or other tomato paste of your choice

3 tablespoons granulated sugar

1 tablespoon Simply Nature Organic Basil Stir-in Paste

1 teaspoon Italian seasoning

1 teaspoon dried oregano

1 teaspoon sea salt

½ teaspoon freshly ground pepper

1. Preheat a medium pot over high heat for 1 minute. Add the butter and olive oil, and heat for 1 to 2 more minutes.

2. Add the onion and garlic, and sauté for 3 to 4 minutes until golden and softened.

3. Stir in the wine, crushed tomatoes, tomato paste, sugar, and seasonings. Reduce the heat to medium. Cook, stirring occasionally, for 20 to 30 minutes. Serve with pasta.

Meat Variation: Add ½ pound pork breakfast sausage (bulk, in a tube) and ½ pound organic ground beef right after sautéing the onion and garlic. Cook, stirring frequently, until the meat is no longer pink, 5 to 8 minutes. Then finish the recipe.

Mushroom Variation: Add 2 (4-ounce) cans of Happy Harvest mushroom pieces and stems or other cans of mushroom pieces and stems of your choice right after sautéing the onion and garlic.

MEDITERRANEAN CHICKEN BAKE

The Mediterranean diet features lots of fresh vegetables, lean meats, and olive oil. This dish features all three.

Yield: 6 servings | Prep Time: 15 minutes | Bake Time: 30 minutes

1 large Kirkwood boneless, skinless chicken breast (2 to 3 pounds), cut into chunks, or other chicken breasts of your choice

6 cups sliced fresh vegetables (onions, zucchini, tomatoes, broccoli...whatever your family loves)

1 teaspoon sea salt

1 teaspoon garlic powder

1 teaspoon onion powder

1 teaspoon dried oregano

2 tablespoons extra-virgin olive oil

1. Preheat the oven to 350°F.

2. Toss all the ingredients together, and then spread them over a large baking dish with raised edges that is lined with either aluminum foil or a silicone baking mat.

3. Bake for 30 minutes.

Notes

• If you want to add feta or Parmesan, remove the baking dish from the oven 10 minutes before the chicken is done, sprinkle about 2 tablespoons of the cheese on top, and finish baking.

CHICKEN PARMIGIANA

ALDI enthusiasts rave about the "red bag" chicken—frozen, breaded chicken breasts. This recipe makes a chicken parmigiana that's better than takeout.

Yield: 6 servings | Prep Time: 5 minutes | Cook Time: 30 minutes

6 Kirkwood Breaded Chicken Breast Fillets (red bag chicken)

1½ cups Red Pasta Sauce (page 76) or other marinara sauce of your choice

1½ cups shredded mozzarella cheese

¾ cup grated Parmesan cheese

1½ teaspoons Italian seasoning

1 tablespoon freshly chopped parsley or basil (optional)

1. Preheat the oven to 400°F.

2. Place the chicken breasts on a baking sheet lined with aluminum foil or a silicone baking mat. Bake for 15 minutes.

3. Flip the chicken breasts over and bake for 10 more minutes.

4. Top each chicken breast with ¼ cup Red Pasta Sauce, ¼ cup shredded mozzarella, 2 tablespoons grated Parmesan cheese, and ¼ teaspoon Italian seasoning. Broil for 3 to 4 minutes until the cheese bubbles.

5. Serve immediately with or without pasta and sprinkle with fresh herbs, if using.

Notes
- Red bag chicken is great for chicken strips, and it's also marvelous for lasagna without noodles and in salads.

CHICKEN, SPINACH, AND MUSHROOM ENCHILADAS

Though these made-from-scratch enchiladas take a little bit of work, they're well worth the effort. The sauce is good enough to eat by itself, but when everything is combined, the result is simply divine.

Yield: 10 filled enchiladas or 5 servings | Prep Time: 15 minutes | Bake Time: 30 minutes

SAUCE:

2 (10-ounce) cans diced tomatoes with green chiles

2 (6-ounce) cans tomato paste

2 cups chicken stock

2 tablespoons honey

2 teaspoons onion powder

2 teaspoons garlic powder

1 teaspoon ground cumin

1 teaspoon paprika

1 teaspoon sea salt

½ teaspoon dried oregano

½ teaspoon ground cinnamon

½ teaspoon Tajín seasoning

½ teaspoon Tajín seasoning

1¼ teaspoons onion powder, divided

1¼ teaspoons garlic powder, divided

1 pound thin chicken breasts (about 2)

olive oil spray

FILLING:

1 (10-ounce) package Season's Choice frozen spinach, thawed, or other spinach of your choice

1 (4-ounce) can mushroom pieces, drained

½ teaspoon salt

¼ teaspoon freshly ground pepper

TO ASSEMBLE:

10 (6-inch) corn or flour tortillas

2 cups shredded Mexican cheese blend or shredded Oaxacan cheese

⅛ teaspoon paprika

⅛ teaspoon ground cumin

⅛ teaspoon dried oregano

sour cream or guacamole, to serve

1. Puree the diced tomatoes with chiles in a food processor fitted with a standard blade or in a high-speed blender, about 30 seconds.

2. Pour the pureed tomato mixture, tomato paste, chicken stock, honey, onion powder, garlic powder, cumin, paprika, salt, dried oregano, cinnamon, and Tajín seasoning into a medium pot. Heat over medium-high heat, whisking constantly, and cook until all the ingredients are blended and warmed through, 5 to 8 minutes. Set aside.

3. Preheat the grill to high. Sprinkle the Tajín seasoning, ¼ teaspoon onion powder, and ¼ teaspoon garlic powder onto both sides of the chicken breasts. Spray the grill with the olive oil. Grill the chicken breasts for 3 to 4 minutes per side. Once cooked, let cool for 5 minutes and then dice into small pieces.

4. Puree the frozen spinach in a food processor fitted with a standard blade or in a high-speed blender, about 1 minute.

5. In a large bowl, stir together the spinach, mushroom pieces, chicken, the remaining 1 teaspoon onion powder, the remaining 1 teaspoon garlic powder, salt, and pepper.

6. To assemble, preheat the oven to 350°F. Pour about half of the sauce in the bottom of a large casserole dish. Place about ⅓ cup of filling onto a corn tortilla, roll, and lay in the casserole dish. Repeat with the remaining tortillas. Top with the cheese and sprinkle with paprika, cumin, and dried oregano. Bake for 30 minutes. Serve with a dollop of sour cream or guacamole.

CHICKEN AND SPINACH CASSEROLE

My kiddo isn't a fan of most casseroles, but he asks for seconds of this one, and he also is equally delighted when it becomes leftovers, which makes me a very happy mama!

Yield: 8 servings | Prep Time: 20 minutes | Bake Time: 30 minutes

1 (8-ounce) package Neufchâtel cheese

1 (10.5-ounce) can Chef's Cupboard mushroom soup or other mushroom soup of your choice

1 (10-ounce) package frozen spinach, thawed

1 cup whole milk

¼ cup Winking Owl Chardonnay or another dry white wine

1 tablespoon dehydrated minced onion

2 teaspoons Stonemill Everything Bagel Seasoning

8 ounces (half a package) Reggano Wide Egg Noodles or other egg noodles of your choice

1 (12-ounce) can chunked chicken

1 (6.5-ounce) can sliced mushrooms

2 cups shredded cheese of choice (shredded Gouda works really, really well)

1 sliced green onion, for garnish (optional)

1. Preheat the oven to 350°F.

2. Place the Neufchâtel cheese, mushroom soup, spinach, milk, wine, dried onion, and bagel seasoning into a food processor fitted with a standard blade. Blend until well mixed, about 1 minute.

3. Bring a large pot of water to a boil. Boil the egg noodles for 7 minutes. Drain.

4. In a large ovenproof casserole dish, stir the cheese and spinach mixture with the chunked chicken and sliced mushrooms. Stir in the cooked noodles.

5. Top with the shredded cheese and bake for 30 minutes. When finished baking, sprinkle with green onion, if desired.

STUFFED CHICKEN BREASTS

Chicken, cheese, and spinach turn into a gourmet feast in this reasonably easy dish.

Yield: 10 to 12 servings (see Notes) | Prep Time: 20 minutes |
Cook Time: about 50 to 55 minutes (45 minutes baking, plus about 6 to 8 minutes to sear)

1 (6-ounce) log Emporium Selection plain goat cheese or other goat cheese of your choice

5 ounces frozen spinach (half a package of frozen spinach)

2 tablespoons Emporium Selection shredded Parmesan or other Parmesan of your choice

1 teaspoon dehydrated minced onion

1 teaspoon garlic powder

1 teaspoon onion powder

1 teaspoon sea salt, plus extra to season

½ teaspoon freshly ground pepper, plus extra to season

4 medium to large Kirkwood chicken breasts or other chicken breasts of your choice

olive oil spray

1. Preheat the oven to 375°F.

2. Place the goat cheese, spinach, Parmesan, dehydrated onion, garlic powder, onion powder, sea salt, and pepper into a food processor fitted with a standard blade. Pulse until well combined. Set aside.

3. Pound each chicken breast until it is about ½-inch thick. Season both sides with sea salt and pepper.

4. Place 2 to 3 tablespoons of the goat cheese and spinach mixture onto one side of a chicken breast. Fold the other side over, and secure by placing 3 or 4 toothpicks through the edges. Repeat with the remaining chicken breasts.

5. Heat a nonstick or cast-iron pan over high heat for 2 minutes. Remove from the heat, spray with olive oil, and sear the stuffed chicken breasts on each side for 3 to 4 minutes, until just turning golden brown. Place the seared chicken breasts on a baking sheet lined with aluminum foil or a silicone baking mat. Spray them with olive oil, and then bake for 45 minutes. The chicken breasts are done when they are cooked to an internal temperature of 165°F, they are no longer pink, and their juices run clear.

Notes

- This recipe serves 10 to 12 people because ALDI's fresh chicken breasts are *huge*. This is great if you have company or if you have a growing teenager or two at home. Or you can just have leftovers, which is also amazing. If you have smaller chicken breasts, modify the recipe by using only 1 to 2 tablespoons of filling to stuff the chicken. You will either stuff more chicken breasts—about 2 to 4 more, depending on size, or you will have some filling leftover to make omelets the next day for breakfast. The filling, by itself, is basically creamy, cheesy spinach.

SWISS STEAK

This was one of my favorite dinners when I was growing up. It's comforting, savory, and warm, and it's also good for company.

Yield: 8 servings | Prep Time: 15 minutes | Cook Time: 3 hours and 15 minutes

3 pounds Black Angus Top Round Steak or other steak of your choice

2 teaspoons Stonemill Minced Garlic in Extra Virgin Olive Oil or minced garlic, divided

1½ teaspoons sea salt, divided

1 teaspoon freshly ground pepper, divided

½ teaspoon garlic salt, divided

½ teaspoon garlic powder, divided

½ teaspoon onion powder, divided

½ teaspoon ground cinnamon, divided

1 tablespoon extra-virgin olive oil

2 pounds fresh baby potatoes

1 pound fresh baby carrots

1 yellow onion, diced

2 (4-ounce) cans Happy Harvest sliced mushrooms or other canned mushrooms of your choice

1 cup Bridge Road Merlot, Bridge Road Vineyards Cabernet Sauvignon, or other dry red wine, divided

1 (28-ounce) can crushed tomatoes

1 (6-ounce) can tomato paste

1 cup beef broth

1 tablespoon chopped fresh parsley (optional)

1. Preheat the oven to 350°F.

2. Season one side of the round steak with 1 teaspoon minced garlic, ½ teaspoon sea salt, and ¼ teaspoon each of pepper, garlic salt, garlic powder, onion powder, and cinnamon. Season the other side with the remaining minced garlic, ½ teaspoon of sea salt, and ¼ teaspoon each of pepper, garlic salt, garlic powder, onion powder, and cinnamon.

3. Heat a large pan for 1 minute over high heat. Add the olive oil, heat for 1 minute, and then sear each side of the round steak for about 3 minutes or until just browned. Remove from the heat and transfer the steak to a large ovenproof roasting pan. Place the potatoes and carrots alongside the steak.

4. Add the onion to the pan, and sauté for 2 to 3 minutes, until just starting to brown. Add the mushrooms, sauté for 1 more minute, and then deglaze the pan with ½ cup of red wine.

5. Whisk in the crushed tomatoes, tomato paste, remaining red wine, beef broth, and remaining salt and pepper.

6. Pour the tomato mixture over the steak, potatoes, and carrots. Cover with aluminum foil, and roast for 3 hours or until the steak is fall-apart tender and cooked to an internal temperature of 145°F. Divide the steak, potatoes, and carrots into about 8 servings. Sprinkle with fresh parsley, if using.

PULLED PORK SLIDERS WITH QUICK COLESLAW

ALDI's meat department rocks, and this version of pulled pork enhances the meat with the fresh taste of peaches.

Yield: 12 servings (2 to 3 sliders per person) | Prep Time: 5 minutes | Cook Time: 4 to 8 hours

1 (15-ounce) can Sweet Harvest Yellow Cling Peaches in Extra Light Syrup or other canned peaches of your choice

4 pounds Roseland pork tenderloin or other pork tenderloin of your choice

½ cup Sunshine Bay Sauvignon Blanc or other white wine of your choice

2 tablespoons dehydrated minced onion

1 tablespoon Stonemill Minced Garlic in Extra Virgin Olive Oil or minced garlic

1 tablespoon Simply Nature Organic Ginger Stir-in Paste

2 teaspoons Stonemill Roasted Garlic Herb Grill Seasoning or garlic salt

1 teaspoon paprika

1 teaspoon sea salt

½ teaspoon freshly ground pepper

1 cup barbecue sauce (optional) (see Notes)

2 tablespoons cornstarch

brioche or Hawaiian sweet rolls, extra barbecue sauce, and Quick Coleslaw (page 90), to serve

1. Puree the peaches in a food processor or blender until smooth.

2. Place all the ingredients (including the barbecue sauce, if using) except for the cornstarch in a slow cooker. Cook on low for 7 hours or on high for 3½ hours.

3. Remove the pork and use a knife and fork to pull the pork apart.

4. Remove 4 tablespoons of liquid from the slow cooker, and in a small bowl, whisk the cornstarch into the liquid. Pour the cornstarch mixture back into the slow cooker. Add the meat back to the slow cooker and stir. Cook for 1 more hour on low or on high for 30 minutes. Remove from the heat, and serve with Hawaiian sweet rolls or brioche rolls and coleslaw.

Notes

• You can add the barbecue sauce right into the slow cooker, or you can pour it into the cooked pork mixture at the very end if you like the barbecue flavor stronger. Or you can leave it out of the recipe—it tastes delicious without it.

• For an extra-smoky flavor, add 1 teaspoon of liquid smoke—just add it in with the rest of the ingredients in the slow cooker.

QUICK COLESLAW

This coleslaw recipe goes great with the pulled pork sliders. It's also delicious on its own.

Yield: about 4 cups or 8 servings—enough to top 12 servings of shredded pork | Prep Time: 15 minutes

3 cups shredded cabbage or
1 package coleslaw mix

¼ red onion, diced

½ red bell pepper, diced

2 carrots, peeled and shredded

1 to 2 tablespoons minced fresh cilantro

¼ cup extra-virgin olive oil

¼ cup apple cider vinegar

2 to 3 tablespoons sugar

1 tablespoon Dijon mustard

2 teaspoons poppy seeds (optional) (see Notes)

1 teaspoon sea salt

1 teaspoon freshly ground pepper

1. Toss all the vegetables together in a medium bowl.

2. In a small bowl, whisk together the olive oil, vinegar, sugar, mustard, poppy seeds, sea salt, and pepper. Pour the dressing over the vegetable mixture, stir, and serve.

Notes

- I haven't seen poppy seeds for sale at ALDI, but they really add to this coleslaw. I recommend, as a substitute, 1 tablespoon of Everything Bagel Seasoning, as it's a mix of poppy seeds and sesame seeds and other goodness. Also, if you use Everything Bagel Seasoning, reduce your sea salt by ½ teaspoon, as EBS also has salt in it.

GROUND TURKEY TACOS

This is a healthier version of ground beef tacos, and it's one of my kiddo's favorite meals (and one of my favorite quick dinners), hands down.

Yield: 8 to 10 tacos or 4 to 5 servings | Cook Time: 15 minutes

1 (1-pound, 3-ounce) package Kirkwood ground turkey or other ground turkey of your choice

1 tablespoon dehydrated minced onion

2 teaspoons ground cumin

1 teaspoon sea salt

1 teaspoon onion powder

1 teaspoon garlic powder

1 teaspoon Tajín seasoning

¼ teaspoon ground cinnamon

1 to 2 tablespoons tomato paste

1 to 2 tablespoons water

8 to 10 taco shells or tortillas

shredded cheese, sour cream, diced tomatoes, diced onions, shredded lettuce, diced avocados, diced olives, salsa, guacamole, and so on, to serve

1. Heat a large nonstick or cast-iron pan over high heat for 1 minute. Add the ground turkey and sauté until it is no longer pink.

2. Add all the seasonings, stir to combine, and then add 1 tablespoon of tomato paste and 1 tablespoon of water. Stir, and if you'd like the turkey mixture to be a little more tomato-y, add the second tablespoon of each.

3. Serve with taco shells and all the taco accompaniments you desire.

Notes
• You can use this same seasoning blend if you're preparing a pound or so of carnitas, chicken breasts, or even shrimp.

BEST BURGERS EVER

A college roommate once showed me her trick of adding fresh grated onion to raw burgers, and ever since then I've been adding it, too. It's a simple step but it makes all the difference!

Yield: 6 burgers or 12 sliders | Prep Time: 20 minutes | Cook Time: 10 to 15 minutes

1 pound Simply Nature grass-fed ground beef or other ground beef of your choice

1 Vidalia onion, peeled and grated

2 tablespoons soy sauce

1 teaspoon garlic powder

½ teaspoon freshly ground pepper

¼ teaspoon ground cinnamon

¾ teaspoon Stonemill Roasted Garlic Herb Grill Seasoning, garlic salt, or sea salt

Hawaiian rolls or brioche buns, to serve

1. Preheat the grill to high.

2. In a bowl, mix together the ground beef, grated onion, soy sauce, garlic powder, pepper, and cinnamon. Form into 6 large patties or 12 small patties and use your thumb to press an indentation into the center of each patty. Sprinkle each patty with ⅛ teaspoon if making six patties or 1/16 teaspoon (just a dash) Roasted Garlic Herb Grill Seasoning, garlic salt, or sea salt if making 12 small patties.

3. Grill each patty for 3 minutes on each side or until cooked to an internal temperature of 160°F.

4. Serve with Hawaiian rolls or brioche buns and whatever toppings you like.

Notes

- If you like cheeseburgers, place half a slice of provolone, cheddar, or Swiss on each burger for the last minute of grilling. Personally, I'm a fan of crumbled blue cheese or goat cheese. You can also top the burgers with grilled onions or mushrooms.

- For extra decadence, mix together a softened stick of butter with 1 teaspoon garlic powder, 1 teaspoon onion powder, and ½ teaspoon sea salt. Then brush each bun with the softened butter before serving.

CHICKEN AND ZUCCHINI CASSEROLE

This is a twist on a squash side dish, but if you add chicken, it becomes an easy weeknight meal. Best of all, if you use the liveGfree stuffing mix, it becomes a delicious gluten-free dish!

Yield: 6 servings | Prep Time: 15 minutes | Cook Time: 30 minutes

3 tablespoons butter, divided

1 Vidalia onion, sliced thin

2 large zucchini, sliced thin

1 large chicken breast (about 8 ounces), cooked and diced

2 cups Simply Nature chicken broth or other chicken broth of your choice

1 (6-ounce) package Chef's Cupboard or liveGfree chicken-flavored stuffing mix or other stuffing mix of your choice

1 (4-ounce) package Neufchâtel cheese

¼ teaspoon sea salt

¼ teaspoon freshly ground pepper

2 cups shredded cheese (cheddar, Gouda, Swiss, mozzarella, or other cheese of your choice)

1. Preheat the oven to 350°F. Grease a 12 x 8-inch casserole dish and set aside.

2. Heat a large pot over high heat for 1 minute. Add 1½ tablespoons of butter and let melt. Reduce the heat to medium, add the onion, and sauté for about 3 minutes or until softened and starting to brown. Add the zucchini slices and the remaining butter, and sauté until softened, 5 to 7 minutes.

3. Add the cooked chicken, broth, stuffing mix, Neufchâtel, sea salt, and pepper, and stir until everything is softened and combined, 2 to 3 minutes. Pour into the prepared dish. Top with the shredded cheese.

4. Bake for 30 minutes or until the cheese is bubbly and starting to brown.

Notes
• This is a great dish for using leftover chicken. You can also easily substitute a can of chicken meat, water drained, for the cooked fresh chicken breast.

TAMALE PIE

Tamales take a lot of work. This tamale pie isn't quite the same as homemade tamales, but it's quite scrumptious, and it freezes really well.

Yield: 12 servings | Prep Time: 15 minutes | Cook Time: 40 minutes

1 pound ground beef

½ white onion, diced

½ green pepper, diced

1 jalapeño pepper, diced

1 (14-ounce) can Happy Harvest diced tomatoes or other tomatoes of your choice

1 (6-ounce) can Happy Harvest tomato paste or other tomato paste of your choice

½ cup water (or beer)

1 teaspoon sea salt

1 teaspoon Tajín seasoning

1 teaspoon ground cumin

1 teaspoon chili powder

¼ teaspoon ground cinnamon

1 teaspoon agave syrup

2 (8.5-ounce) boxes Jiffy cornbread mix or other cornbread mix of your choice

2 eggs

½ cup 2 percent or nonfat milk

1 cup Happy Harvest creamed corn or other creamed corn of your choice

canola oil spray

1½ cups Happy Farms shredded Mexican cheese blend or other cheese blend of your choice

1. Preheat the oven to 400°F.

2. Heat a large nonstick or cast-iron skillet over high heat for 1 to 2 minutes. Add the ground beef and sauté until no longer pink.

3. Add the onion and sauté for about 5 minutes, until cooked through. Then add the green pepper and jalapeño pepper, and sauté until cooked. Add the diced tomatoes, tomato paste, and water, stir until well combined, and then add the seasonings and agave syrup. Cook for about 5 minutes, until everything is warm and well mixed.

4. Meanwhile, in a large bowl, mix together the cornbread mix, eggs, milk, and creamed corn.

5. Spray a 9½ x 9½-inch pan with the canola oil. Pour the meat and vegetable mixture into the bottom of the pan. Spread the cornbread mixture on top. Top with shredded cheese and bake for 20 minutes.

CHEESE FONDUE

There is nothing so delicious on a cold winter's night as a steamy, cheesy pot of fondue. Mmm... it's just so warm and satisfying. Though the dish might seem sophisticated, if your kids love cheese, they'll probably enjoy this!

Yield: 4 servings | Prep Time: 5 minutes | Cook Time: 15 minutes

3 cups Emporium Selection Swiss and Gruyère shredded cheese or other Swiss cheese blend of your choice

1 teaspoon all-purpose flour

1 clove garlic

1½ cups Broken Clouds chardonnay or other dry white wine of your choice

1 tablespoon freshly squeezed lemon juice

½ teaspoon ground nutmeg

¼ teaspoon freshly ground pepper

fresh bread, cubed (preferably French loaves)

1. In a large bowl, dredge the cheese and flour together. Set aside.

2. Rub the garlic clove all around the inside of a medium pot. Discard.

3. Pour the wine into the pot and heat over medium-high heat until it is hot but not boiling. Stir in the lemon juice. Then add the cheese and flour mixture, a handful at a time, stirring constantly until the cheese has melted and combines with the wine into a light, sauce-like texture. Keep stirring until the mixture begins to bubble. Stir in the nutmeg and pepper.

4. Remove from the heat, and if you have a fondue pot, place it on a lighted burner or over a Sterno. Serve with bread and long forks. (See Notes.)

Notes

- If you don't have a fondue pot or anything to keep the pot warm, you have two options. You can put the pot on a trivet, or you can pour the fondue into a large, microwave-safe bowl. If the fondue starts hardening, then just stick it into the microwave for 30 to 60 seconds to soften it.

- If you want to make this more kid friendly, use shredded cheddar cheese, and if you're doing a tailgate party, use cheddar instead of Swiss and replace the wine with an equal amount of beer.

GRILLED PORK CHOPS WITH APPLES AND ONIONS

Pork and apples go together like peanut butter and jelly. Add in onion and you've got yourself a winning combination.

Yield: 4 servings | Prep Time: 15 minutes | Cook Time: 20 minutes

4 bone-in, center-cut pork chops

1¼ teaspoons sea salt, divided

¼ teaspoon garlic powder

¼ teaspoon onion powder

¼ teaspoon freshly ground pepper

canola oil spray

2 apples (green or red), peeled, cored, cut in half, and rubbed with ¼ fresh lemon

1 onion (red or yellow), peeled and cut in half

1 tablespoon butter

2 teaspoons extra-virgin olive oil

1 tablespoon apple cider vinegar

1 tablespoon real maple syrup

fresh rosemary, for garnish (optional)

1. Preheat the grill to high.

2. Season both sides of the pork chops with 1 teaspoon sea salt, garlic powder, onion powder, and pepper. Set aside.

3. Spray the grill with canola oil. Place the apple and onion halves on the grill. Grill for 3 to 4 minutes per side. Remove from the grill and set aside.

4. Grill the pork chops on each side for 3 to 4 minutes.

5. While the pork chops are grilling, slice the grilled apples and onions. Heat a medium nonstick pan over high heat. Melt the butter in the pan, add the olive oil, and then sauté the apple and onion slices for about 3 minutes. Pour in the apple cider vinegar and maple syrup. Cook until the apple cider vinegar is almost evaporated and the onion is caramelized, about 5 minutes. Season with the remaining sea salt.

6. Serve the pork chops topped with the grilled apples, the grilled onions, and the fresh rosemary, if using.

Notes
- If you have the time and the inclination, ALDI's pork chops become even tastier (and juicier) if you brine them. A simple brine is 2 to 3 cups water, ⅓ cup salt, ⅓ cup maple syrup or brown sugar, plus spices or citrus peels or both. I'm fond of putting in 1 tablespoon of peppercorns, a bay leaf or two, fresh herbs from my garden, and the peel of a lemon or an orange. I whisk everything together, put it in a container with the raw pork chops, and let them brine for 30 minutes to overnight in the refrigerator.

Chapter Five

DESSERTS

CANNOLI DIP

My sister Karen makes this incredibly addictive dessert dip packed with all the good flavors of a cannoli. It's so delicious you'll have a hard time not eating the whole thing in one sitting!

Yield: 3 cups or about 12 (¼-cup) servings | Prep Time: 5 minutes

1 cup Special Emporium whole milk ricotta cheese or other ricotta cheese of your choice

1 (8-ounce) package Happy Farms cream cheese or other cream cheese of your choice

¾ cup powdered sugar

1 teaspoon vanilla extract

1 (10-ounce) package chocolate mini-chips

graham crackers, cookies, or fresh fruit, to serve

1. Place the ricotta cheese, cream cheese, powdered sugar, and vanilla extract in a food processor fitted with a standard blade. Blend on low for 1 to 2 minutes until smooth and creamy.

2. Stir in the chocolate mini-chips. Serve with graham crackers, cookies, or fresh fruit.

Notes

- If you have some sweet brandy, chocolate liqueur, or Tuaca (a vanilla-and-spice-flavored sweet Italian brandy), add 1 tablespoon for extra flavor.
- If you're looking to make a slightly healthier version, you can sub low-fat cottage cheese for the ricotta, and you can sub Neufchâtel cheese for the cream cheese. It's still scrumptious!
- This also makes a toothsome filling for a layer cake.

CHERRY SURPRISE CUPCAKES WITH DARK CHOCOLATE GANACHE

These cupcakes are so delicious that while I am frosting them with ganache, my husband and son are eating the ones that I've just frosted. They're really that tantalizing, so if you want to serve them for a party or guests, make them when no one else is around.

Yield: 12 servings | Prep Time: 20 minutes | Cook Time: 25 minutes

CAKE:

½ cup heavy cream

1 stick unsalted butter

4 eggs

1 tablespoon vanilla extract

1 (15.25-ounce) Baker's Corner Classic Yellow Cake Mix, 1 (15-ounce) box liveGfree Gluten Free Yellow Baking Mix, or other cake mix of your choice

1 cup or about half of 1 (21-ounce) can Baker's Corner cherry pie filling or other cherry pie filling of your choice (reserve the rest for other uses, such as topping ice cream or oatmeal)

DARK CHOCOLATE GANACHE:

½ cup heavy cream

¾ cup dark chocolate chips

CAKE

1. Preheat the oven to 350°F. In a standing mixer, pour in the heavy cream, butter, eggs, and vanilla extract. Beat on low until well combined, about 2 minutes. Add the cake mix and beat until smooth, about 2 minutes.

2. Line a 12-cup muffin pan with cupcake liners. Place about 1 rounded tablespoon of cake mixture into the bottom of each cupcake liner. (If you are not using cupcake liners, grease each muffin tin.)

3. Place ½ rounded tablespoon of cherry pie filling (2 to 3 cherries plus sauce) in the middle of each cupcake. Top with 1 rounded tablespoon of cake mixture, being careful to seal the cherry filling in between the layers.

4. Bake for 25 minutes or until golden brown on top. Remove the cupcakes from the oven and let cool for about 5 minutes so that you can remove them from the muffin pan.

DARK CHOCOLATE GANACHE

1. Microwave the heavy cream in a microwave-safe bowl for 30 to 45 seconds, being careful that it doesn't bubble over.

2. Pour the cream over the chocolate chips, which should be in a medium microwave-safe bowl. Whisk until smooth, about 5 minutes. If a few chips refuse to completely melt, microwave the ganache mixture for 10 to 15 seconds and whisk until smooth.

3. Dip the cupcakes into the ganache mixture. Do this by holding each cupcake gently and swirling it into the ganache. You will have some ganache left over, which can be used as a dip for cookies or as a drizzle for fruit. You can also use the ganache as a hot fudge sauce on ice cream.

POOP EMOJI CUPCAKES WITH MILK CHOCOLATE FROSTING

My sister Karen shared this recipe with me, as her daughter Briana thinks poop emojis are so funny. Well, these cupcakes are funny to look at, inviting to eat, and easy to make. The perfect trifecta in a kid's dessert.

Yield: 12 cupcakes | Prep Time: 10 minutes | Cook Time: 60 minutes (20 to 30 minutes cooking time, plus another 30 to 40 minutes to frost and assemble poop eyes)

CAKE BATTER:

1 (16-ounce) package Baker's Corner chocolate baking mix, liveGfree gluten-free brownie mix, or other cake mix or brownie mix of your choice

1 (3.9-ounce) package Baker's Corner chocolate or vanilla instant pudding mix or other pudding mix of your choice

1 cup heavy cream

½ cup milk chocolate chips

3 eggs

½ cup unsalted butter, melted

1 tablespoon vanilla extract

FROSTING:

1 cup milk chocolate chips

1 (8-ounce) package Neufchâtel cheese

½ cup butter

1 cup powdered sugar

1 teaspoon vanilla extract

POOP EYES:

24 milk chocolate chips

24 miniature marshmallows (optional)

Baker's Corner vanilla frosting (optional)

1. Preheat the oven to 350°F.

2. Whisk all the cake batter ingredients together. Line a 12-cupcake tin with liners and divide the batter among them.

3. Bake for 20 to 30 minutes.

4. While the cake is baking, place the chocolate chips for the frosting in a microwave-safe container. Microwave on high for about 1 minute, and then stir until all the chips are melted.

5. Place the Neufchâtel cheese, butter, powdered sugar, and vanilla extract in a high-speed mixer, and mix on high until well blended.

6. Pour in the melted chocolate chips, and whip until well blended.

7. When the cupcakes are finished baking, remove them from the oven and let cool for at least 10 minutes. To frost, fill a pastry bag fitted with a medium star, and swirl the frosting on in the shape of a poop. If you don't have a pastry bag, you can pour frosting into a zip-top plastic bag. Seal, snip off a corner of the bag, and gently squeeze the frosting in the shape of a poop emoji out of that opening.

8. To make the poop eyes, use clean hands to press each chocolate chip, pointed side down, into each marshmallow, and then place onto a frosted cupcake. You can also get creative with some Baker's Corner vanilla frosting or mini marshmallows for a more detailed face!

BROWNIE ORANGES

Though it may be a bit fussy to carve out oranges, this recipe turns a regular pan of brownies into a fancy dessert. Plus, you'll have a healthy snack of freshly peeled oranges to eat while you wait for the brownies to bake!

Yield: 12 servings | Prep Time: 45 minutes | Cook Time: 30 minutes

12 navel oranges

¼ cup sugar

¼ cup coconut flour or almond flour

¼ cup Baker's Corner unsweetened cocoa powder or other cocoa powder of your choice

¼ teaspoon baking soda

3 large eggs

1½ teaspoons vanilla extract

1 stick (8 ounces) unsalted butter

1 (10-ounce) bag Baker's Corner Dark Chocolate Morsels or semisweet chocolate chips or other chocolate chips of your choice

zest of 1 orange

sugar, for sprinkling

1. Preheat the oven to 350°F.

2. Using a paring knife, slice the top off one orange. Then, using both the knife and a spoon, scoop out the interior of the orange, being careful not to tear the skin. Repeat with each orange, placing each orange into a muffin tin. Reserve the orange fruit for another use, but save the tops.

3. In a large bowl, whisk together the sugar, coconut flour, cocoa powder, and baking soda. Whisk in the eggs and vanilla extract.

4. In a microwave-safe bowl, melt the butter on high for 1 minute. Whisk into the batter.

5. In a microwave-safe bowl, melt the chocolate chips for 30 seconds, whisk, then return to the microwave to finish melting, about 30 to 60 seconds.

6. Whisk the chocolate into the batter, stir in the orange zest, and then divide the batter evenly among the 12 hollowed-out oranges. Fill each orange only about halfway—do not overfill.

7. Bake for 30 minutes. Let cool for about 3 minutes.

8. While the desserts are cooling, turn the broiler on high. Lay the orange tops on a cookie sheet, interior side up, and sprinkle with sugar (about 1 tablespoon). Broil for 1 to 2 minutes to caramelize the sugar. Remove from the heat, and top each baked orange brownie.

QUICK FROZEN YOGURT

If you love frozen yogurt but are trying to eat healthier, this quick, three-ingredient dessert is for you.

Yield: 1½ cups or 1 to 2 servings | Prep Time: 0 | Make Time: 5 minutes

2 cups Season's Choice frozen fruit, such as strawberries or tropical fruit blend, or other frozen fruit of your choice

1 (6-ounce) container Friendly Farms light vanilla yogurt or other yogurt of your choice

½ teaspoon vanilla extract

1. Place all the ingredients in a blender fitted with a standard blade.

2. Blend until completely smooth, about 5 minutes.

Notes

- This has the consistency of soft-serve yogurt. If you like it richer, choose a Greek-style or full-fat yogurt. If you prefer it with a more frozen consistency, put it in the freezer for 30 to 60 minutes. And if you're partial to sweetness, add 1 to 2 teaspoons of sugar.

CHOCOLATE CHIP BANANA BREAD

This could fit in the breakfast chapter, but it's so yummy, it's more like a dessert.

Yield: 8 slices | Prep Time: 15 minutes | Bake Time: 60 minutes

¼ cup unsalted butter, softened

½ cup sugar

2 eggs

2 overripe bananas

1 cup milk

1 tablespoon vanilla extract

1½ cups all-purpose flour or flour of your choice

½ cup Simply Nature Milled Flax Seeds or other ground flax seeds of your choice

1 tablespoon baking powder

1 teaspoon ground cinnamon

½ cup chopped walnuts or pecans

1 cup Baker's Corner Dark Chocolate Morsels or semisweet chocolate chips or other chocolate chips of your choice

1. Preheat the oven to 350°F. Grease and flour a 10 x 5-inch loaf pan.

2. In a large bowl, and using an electric mixer on medium speed, blend the butter with the sugar. Add the eggs and bananas. Add the milk and vanilla extract.

3. Then add the flour, flax seeds, baking powder, and cinnamon. Stir in the chopped nuts and chocolate chips. Pour into the prepared loaf pan.

4. Bake for 60 minutes or until a toothpick inserted into the center comes out clean.

Notes

• For a more tropical flavor, add 1 tablespoon of rum and ½ cup of sweetened coconut flakes to the batter during step 3.

CAKE MIX SUGAR COOKIES

This is the perfect recipe to have on hand whenever you need an emergency batch of cookies—like when your kiddos tell you at the last minute that it's their turn to bring treats to scouts or the baseball game. It's kid-approved, easy, and most important, it won't have you up all night baking.

Yield: 36 to 40 cookies | Prep Time: 15 minutes | Cook Time: 11 to 12 minutes

1 stick Countryside Creamery Unsalted Butter or other unsalted butter of your choice, softened

1 (15.25-ounce) Baker's Corner Classic Yellow Cake Mix, 1 (15-ounce) box liveGfree Gluten Free Yellow Baking Mix, or other cake mix of your choice

2 eggs

2 teaspoons vanilla extract

zest of 1 lemon

½ cup sugar

1. Preheat the oven to 350°F. Grease two cookie sheets or line them with a silicone baking mat.

2. In a standard mixer, combine the butter with the cake mix. Add the eggs, vanilla extract, and lemon zest. Mix until well combined.

3. Form balls about the size of a quarter. Pour the sugar into a shallow bowl, and then roll each cookie ball in sugar. Place the cookie balls on the cookie sheets, spaced at least ¾ of an inch apart. Using the back of a cup, gently flatten them.

4. Bake for 11 to 12 minutes, until just starting to brown around the edges. Remove from the heat. Let cool for 5 minutes on cookie sheets, and then remove them to cool on a cookie rack.

Notes

• If you like your cookies chewy, bake them for 11 to 12 minutes. But if you like them crispy, bake them for 13 to 14 minutes, being careful not to overbake them.

• If your family prefers chocolate chips, eliminate the lemon zest and add 1 cup of chocolate chips, pressing them into the cookies after you've flattened them onto the cookie sheets.

HOMEMADE HOT FUDGE SAUCE

Homemade hot fudge sauce just makes ice cream sundaes taste so much better.

Yield: 4 servings | Cook Time: 3 minutes

½ cup Baker's Corner Dark Chocolate Morsels or other chocolate chips of your choice

2 tablespoons heavy whipping cream or whole milk (see Notes)

ice cream of choice, to serve

whipped cream (optional), to serve

nuts (optional), to serve

cookies or brownies (optional), to serve

1. In a microwave-safe bowl, melt the chocolate chips on high heat for 1 minute.

2. Whisk the chips, which should be melty but not yet fully melted. After the chips are whisked and completely melted (if they aren't yet melted, microwave them in 10-second increments) (see Notes), whisk in the heavy whipping cream or whole milk.

3. Pour the hot fudge sauce over your ice cream of choice, and then top with whipped cream and nuts, if desired. Each serving of this hot fudge sauce is about 2 tablespoons. Serve with cookies or brownies, if desired.

Notes

- Heavy whipping cream makes for a richer sauce, but you can use whole milk or a nondairy milk. The sauce will not be as thick, but it will still taste delicious.

- It should take only about 1 minute to melt ½ cup of chips, but every microwave is different. When I make hot fudge sauce, I melt the chips for 1 minute and then whisk them. As they whisk, they melt. Sometimes, if I overpour the chips (which does happen), I need to add another 10 to 20 seconds of microwaving. If some chunks still aren't melting, microwave them in 10-second increments and whisk between increments. Also, do *not* allow any water to drip onto the chips—that will cause your chocolate to seize or get icky. If that happens, toss it and start again.

CHOCOLATE PEANUT BUTTER ICE CREAM PIE

If you love ALDI's Choceur Peanut Butter Cups, then you'll love this recipe.

Yield: 8 servings | Prep Time: 20 minutes | Freeze Time: 4 hours

3 cups Belmont Vanilla Bean Ice Cream, slightly softened (see Notes) or other ice cream of your choice

1 cup peanut butter

1 (6-ounce) Baker's Corner Graham Cracker Pie Crust or other 9-inch graham cracker pie crust of your choice

1 cup milk chocolate or dark chocolate chips

1 cup heavy cream plus 3 tablespoons, divided

½ cup marshmallow fluff (see Notes)

½ cup Choceur Peanut Butter Cups or other peanut butter cups of your choice, quartered

1. Mix together the ice cream and peanut butter using a standard mixer until well combined. Pour the ice cream mixture into the graham cracker pie crust. Place in the freezer.

2. Place the chocolate chips into a microwave-safe bowl. Microwave on high for 60 seconds, then whisk the chips until melted. Whisk in 3 tablespoons of heavy cream. Remove the pie from the freezer. Spread the ganache on top of the pie, and return the pie to the freezer.

3. Whip the remaining heavy cream in the mixer until light and fluffy. Pour in the marshmallow fluff and whip until combined. Remove the pie from the freezer, and spread the heavy cream–marshmallow fluff mixture on top of the pie. Top with peanut butter cups.

4. Freeze for at least 4 hours.

Notes

- The ice cream will soften if you leave it outside the freezer for 15 minutes (or, in my case, the time it takes me to drive home from ALDI!).

- ALDI's marshmallow fluff is a seasonal item, sold only before the winter holidays. If it's out of season and you don't want to go to another store, you can take 1 cup of marshmallows and 1 tablespoon of corn syrup, honey, or agave syrup, and microwave them together on high for 30 to 45 seconds. Whisk the ingredients together, and you've got a quick marshmallow fluff. You can also leave out the marshmallow fluff, and instead just add 1 tablespoon of powdered sugar and 1 teaspoon of vanilla extract to the heavy cream.

- My sister does a more complicated version of this recipe using the Benton's chocolate peanut butter cookies from ALDI—she mashes them up in a food processor, and then combines the mashed cookies with butter to form a peanut buttery and chocolatey crust.

Conversions

VOLUME

US	US Equivalent	Metric
1 tablespoon (3 teaspoons)	½ fluid ounce	15 milliliters
¼ cup	2 fluid ounces	60 milliliters
⅓ cup	3 fluid ounces	90 milliliters
½ cup	4 fluid ounces	120 milliliters
⅔ cup	5 fluid ounces	150 milliliters
¾ cup	6 fluid ounces	180 milliliters
1 cup	8 fluid ounces	240 milliliters
2 cups	16 fluid ounces	480 milliliters

WEIGHT

US	Metric
½ ounce	15 grams
1 ounce	30 grams
2 ounces	60 grams
¼ pound	115 grams
⅓ pound	150 grams
½ pound	225 grams
¾ pound	350 grams
1 pound	450 grams

TEMPERATURE

Fahrenheit (°F)	Celsius (°C)	Fahrenheit (°F)	Celsius (°C)
70°F	20°C	220°F	105°C
100°F	40°C	240°F	115°C
120°F	50°C	260°F	125°C
130°F	55°C	280°F	140°C
140°F	60°C	300°F	150°C
150°F	65°C	325°F	165°C
160°F	70°C	350°F	175°C
170°F	75°C	375°F	190°C
180°F	80°C	400°F	200°C
190°F	90°C	425°F	220°C
200°F	95°C	450°F	230°C

Acknowledgments

The author would like to enthusiastically thank her incredible agent, the amazing Marilyn Allen, who has been with her every step of the way on her journey as an author. She would also like to express her extreme gratitude and appreciation for her phenomenal editor, Claire Sielaff, as well as the whole team at Ulysses Press, including Kathy Kaiser, Renee Rutledge, and Tyanni Niles. She also thanks her family for their tireless support, especially her husband, Kyle Edwards, and their son, Quinn.

About the Author

Jeanette Hurt is an award-winning author of 15 books on food and drink, and she is a recipe developer for both publications and agencies. She regularly contributes to numerous magazines, including *Forbes*, *Huffington Post*, *Eating Well*, and *Chicago Health*. When she's not writing or developing recipes, you can find her walking along the lakefront with her family and their dog in Milwaukee, Wisconsin. Visit her website www.jeanettehurt.com, follow her on Twitter @byJeanetteHurt, or follow her on Facebook: facebook.com/byjeanettehurt.